MW00714574

While this book is intended as a general information resource and all care has been taken in compiling the contents, this book does not take account of individual circumstances. Proper safety equipment should be used especially when starting out — it will help to prevent injuries and may help you to improve more quickly too. The author and the publisher cannot be held responsible for any claim or action that may arise from reliance on the information contained in this book.

CORBIN HARRIS'
ULTIMATE GUIDE TO
SKATEBOARDING

I remember the day my brother came home raving about the new skatepark he'd just seen in **Taren Point.** We were so excited we jumped on our BMXs and rode down there like maniacs. We pulled up on our bikes and checked it out through the fence. It was a skateboarder's dream: an undercover warehouse full of perfect new ramps. And the fact Jake Brown and other up-and-coming pros of the day were skating it, made it look even radder. Not skating wasn't even an option and this park soon became my second home.

Looking back I'm grateful for those moments that inspired me to skate and keep on skating, so I could reach the point I'm at today. It got me thinking; there are plenty of potential skateboarders out there, in need of the information or inspiration to get started. If this sounds like you, then this book might be just what you're looking for. I hope you're stoked on it.

Enough chat, let's skate!

MY FIRST BOARD: 1988

Sequence: Andrew Peters

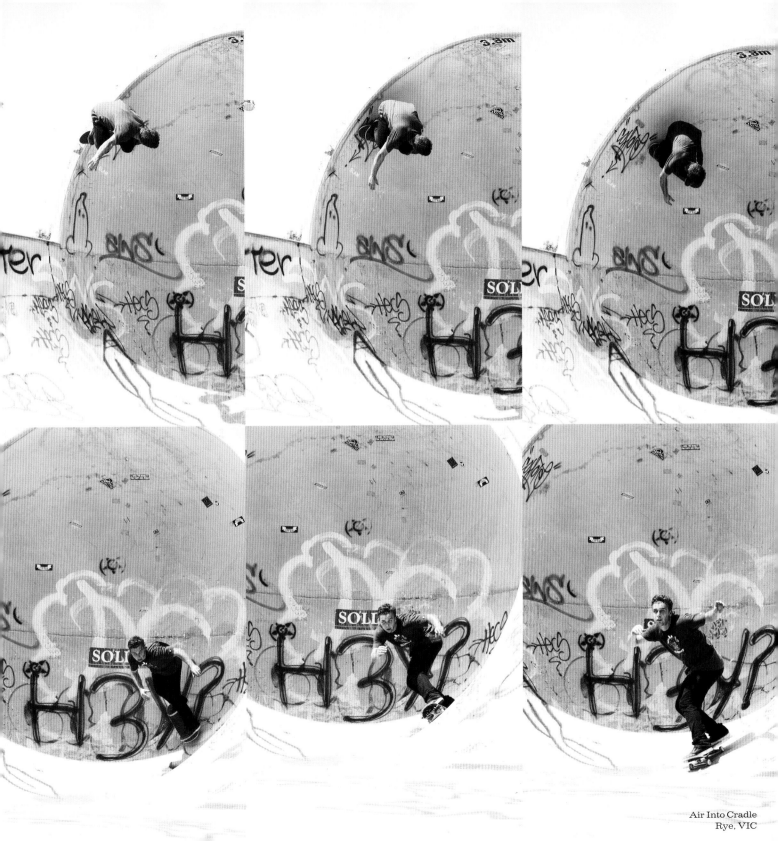

Air Into Cradle
Rye, VIC

Photo: Steve Gourlay

Photo: Young Vo

Lien Air
Woodgate, QLD

CONTENTS

"*A skateboard* is one of the best toys in the world. It's what you do with it that can make it a hobby, a sport, or even a *career*."

GETTING EQUIPPED

CHOOSING AND PUTTING TOGETHER
THE ULTIMATE SET-UP

A skateboard is one of the best toys in the world and it's what you do with it that can make it either a hobby, a sport or a career—just like a footy, a surfboard or a tennis racket. Unlike these things, though, skateboards have a few more parts so they're way more fun to play with! Once you're into it, trust me, you could spend hours tinkering with your set-up—replacing your bearings, rotating your wheels, tightening and untightening your trucks—all in the quest for the perfect set-up. Chances are you'll get it right and then you'll accidentally snap your board—hey, these things happen! The following section includes my tips on how to choose each piece of equipment and how to put your skateboard together—and then the fun part of how you use it is up to you.

CHOOSING THE DECK

Most deck companies produce the same range of standard board widths ranging from 7.5–8.5 inches. From there, however, the differences can vary in length, concave, nose and tail shape, type of plywood, glues and of course the graphics.

Sometimes these variations are so subtle it's not until you actually try a new board, say with a steeper tail, that you realise that it works better for your style.

What is important to one person might not be to another, so the science of it really comes down to—if it feels right under your feet, it probably is.

As a general guide, here are some points to consider when buying a new board:

• If you're smaller in stature and weight, a board between 7.5" and 7.75" wide is a good place to start.

• Conversely, a larger framed skater is likely to feel more comfortable on an 8"–8.25" board with a longer wheelbase.

• The longer the nose and tail length, the better the board for sliding, but it may be harder to ollie.

• A shorter wheelbase will help your board turn faster, whilst a longer wheelbase will help maintain stability and speed.

I started out skating 7.5" boards but now tend to ride an 8.125", which I like for skating bigger transition, as well as I like to have more room for my feet on the board. You'll soon work out what works for you.

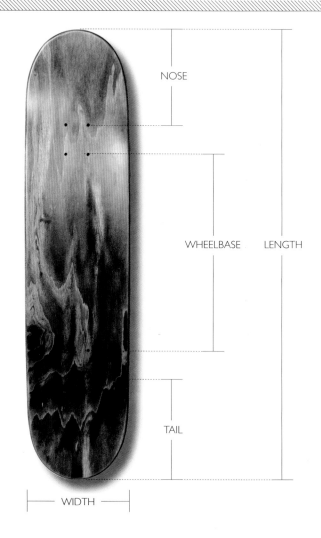

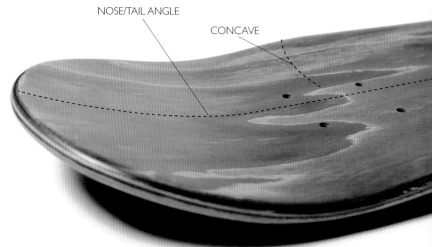

TRUCK WIDTH

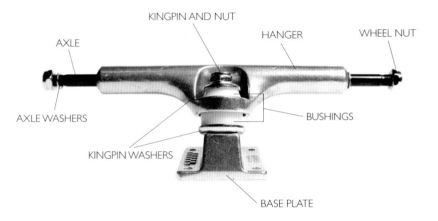

KINGPIN AND NUT

HANGER

WHEEL NUT

AXLE

AXLE WASHERS

BUSHINGS

KINGPIN WASHERS

BASE PLATE

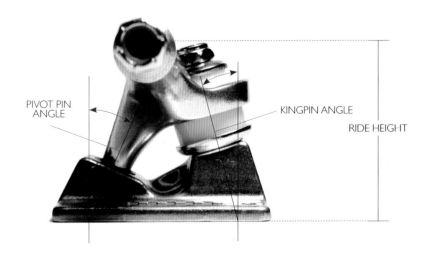

PIVOT PIN ANGLE

KINGPIN ANGLE

RIDE HEIGHT

CHOOSING TRUCKS

When choosing trucks the first point to consider is buying trucks to suit the width of your board. As a general rule, your wheels when mounted on your trucks should sit just inside, or sit flush with the edges of your board.

Once you've narrowed down your truck width, you still might be faced with alternatives, as trucks can also vary in what they're made from, their weight, ride heights, and kingpin and pivot pin angles. I'll give you a basic breakdown, although experience on your board will be the best teacher when it comes to trucks.

MATERIALS
Trucks are generally made of aluminium which is quite a soft metal, so it will grind well on concrete ledges and pool coping but it wears quickly. Titanium trucks are more expensive but last longer due to the titanium being harder and therefore more durable.

RIDE HEIGHT
Some truck brands will use the word 'lows'—referring to a lower ride height. This means the axle is closer to your deck, offering a lower centre of gravity. This can be good for skating flat ground and ledges, where you can sacrifice the turning response for greater board control.

Trucks referring to a 'mid' ride height are good all-rounders, which will suit most wheels from 50mm through to 55mm without fear of wheel bite. [When your wheels rub/grab on your deck when turning or landing.]

'Highs', as you would guess, are trucks used for larger diameter wheels, such as for vert boards or cruiser boards.

TRUCK GEOMETRY
Truck geometry refers to the angle of the kingpin and pivot pin, which both affect the stability and turning ability of the truck.

To help you understand how the truck's angles might impact your skateboarding, imagine an extreme scenario, where the kingpin was nearly vertical—the truck would be hard to turn but would be very stable. Conversely, if the kingpin was on a very mellow angle the truck would be very responsive to turning but wouldn't be as stable. Then add in there variations on the pivot pin angle and you have an endless number of combinations and effects!

CHOOSING WHEELS

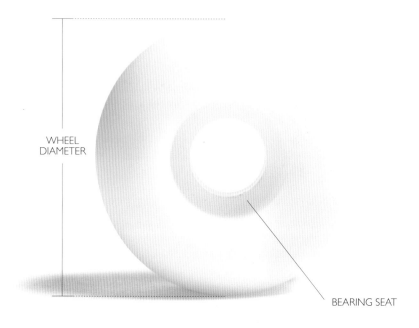

WHEEL DIAMETER

BEARING SEAT

Your choice of wheels will also relate to your trucks, which you probably realise by now, so I can assume that you won't try and put 58mm wheels with low trucks on your street set-up. If you get confused, ask around at the skatepark, or at your local skateshop; you're not expected to know everything straight away.

WHEEL DIAMETER

Wheel diameter is the most obvious point of difference when comparing wheels. There have been various trends throughout the years, but generally 50mm–54mm wheels are a good size for skating street and parks. Larger wheels in the 55mm–58mm range are great for getting over large coping and maintaining high speeds in bowls, and even larger wheels, ranging 60mm–64mm, are normally used for skating massive vert ramps. Wheels over this size would normally be used for downhill or cruiser boards.

RIDING SURFACE

The riding surface is the area of the wheel that actually connects with the ground. In comparing wheels you're likely to discover that one set of 54mm wheels could have a different width riding surface to another set of 54mm wheels. The riding surface greatly affects traction—the wider the riding surface the more traction you'll get and vice versa. The adverse effect of this is that with a wider riding surface you'll also get more friction, which will slow you down and make it harder to slide.

DUROMETER

Wheel hardness is less obvious to the eye but is also a major part of selecting your wheels. The urethane compound that makes up the wheels is measured on a scale called an 'A' Durometer scale.

    To cut a long story short, the lower the Durometer number the softer the wheel and the higher the number the harder the wheel. For example, a 75A 70mm wheel would be large and soft, great for a longboard/cruiser, whereas a 97A 52mm wheel would be great for general purpose street skating.

    I have a few set-ups with different wheels for different situations. My 54mm wheels are perfect for all types of skating —street, park or bowl. If I was skating street all the time I would go down to a 53mm, which I think feels better for flips. Riding vert or big transition I go up to a 58mm wheel or even 60mm on a 13ft transition.

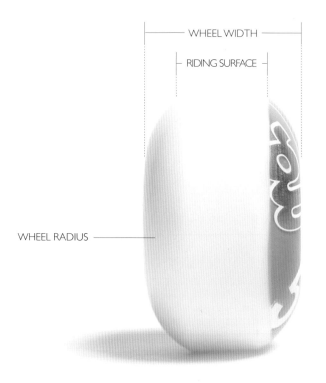

WHEEL WIDTH

RIDING SURFACE

WHEEL RADIUS

STANDARD BEARING

BEARING COVER

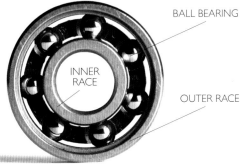

BALL BEARING

INNER RACE

OUTER RACE

CHOOSING BEARINGS

Your bearings will take a lot of punishment, so I think a good rule of thumb when selecting bearings is to buy the best you can afford. You still need to look after them to keep them working well—even expensive bearings aren't immune to dirt, dust and water.

To help you differentiate, the quality of metal bearings is an ABEC rating. This refers to the tolerance at the manufacturing stage, which goes on to affect how they perform. The tolerance relates to the gap between the ball bearing and the inner and outer race. The more precise the tolerance the longer and faster the bearing will spin. The closer the tolerance the higher the ABEC rating. You might think, well I'll just get the highest ABEC rating I possibly can … well think again. The closer the tolerance the more heat that is generated, therefore possibly causing your bearings to wear out faster! You'll probably find anything from ABEC 3–7 at your local skate shop, so if you can't decide head somewhere in the middle with an ABEC 5.

Two types of bearings without ABEC ratings are titanium and ceramic bearings. They are both more expensive and their materials and technology explain why.

TITANIUM BEARINGS
Titanium is an extremely hard metal so it doesn't wear as much as other metal bearings. It can also be machined with greater precision, so everything is bound to run smoother. I use either ABEC 5s or titanium bearings, which both feel very much the same to me, although the titaniums hold out longer.

CERAMIC BEARINGS
These are completely made from a special, super hard ceramic material so there are no metal parts at all. The ceramic doesn't heat up like metal, so therefore it doesn't expand, so there is less friction within the bearing. These are way more durable, yet I tend not to use them because they feel too hard under my feet. It might sound strange saying that but after riding for a few years you'll know what I mean, and you might even disagree!

SPACERS

WASHERS

CHOOSING HARDWARE

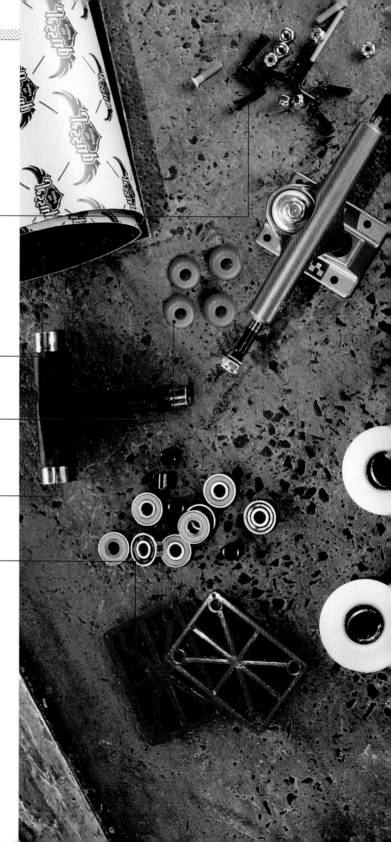

DECK BOLTS

Bolts or mounting hardware come in tons of different packaging but they're generally the same. The length of the bolt will be determined by a couple of things, ie:

1. A short bolt like 1.0" will work well for just mounting your trucks straight to your deck.

2. A 13/4" bolt will work well if mounting your truck onto your deck with a 1/2" riser pad to give you more ride height.

Most bolts have a hex head and will come with an Allen key, while the nuts will have a 'nyloc' insert that stops them vibrating loose.

GRIP TAPE

Grip tape comes in a few different grades set apart by the brand. Some brands have a heavier, rougher texture for a more solid grip while others have a finer texture and are less grippy.

BUSHINGS

Your trucks will come with standard bushings, but you can replace them depending on whether you want them harder or softer. Soft bushings will help your trucks respond and turn quickly, whereas hard bushings will give you stability.

TRUCK TOOL

Trust me, you'll always be in need of a truck tool, so make your life easier by investing in a good quality tool. Keep an eye on it, though, as they tend to go missing when your mates are around!

RISER PADS

Riser pads are plastic pads that sit between your board and your truck to increase the ride height of your trucks. They generally come in 1/8", 1/4" and 1/2" thicknesses. If you ride bigger wheels, like on a cruiser or a longboard, these will help to give your wheels more clearance from the deck [therefore avoiding wheel bite].

GRIPPING YOUR BOARD

Peel the backing paper from the grip tape, and for your own sanity try and start with a flat piece of grip in the first place—it will make it way easier to place it on the board.

Have your board on a good flat surface and line the grip up over the top of your board before placing it down on the board's surface. If you place it right you'll have about 1cm of overhang around the sides.

Working from the centre of the board out to the edges, press the grip down and push out any air bubbles.

You can then use the backing paper over the top of the grip and work from the centre out to the edges to smooth it down properly.

To trim the excess grip from around the board it's best to score the area that needs to be cut. That way you can follow the line when you're cutting and the excess comes away from the board easier.

You can use any smooth metal-type tool to score the edges—the hanger of your truck or a screwdriver —and follow it around the top edge of your board til you can see the outline of the whole board.

Using a Stanley knife, make an initial cut into the excess grip on the side. Do this towards the tip of the board as it's easier to start trimming in a straight line down the sides instead of starting around the nose or tail.

Now, putting the Stanley knife between the cut you've made, position it so the blade is facing upwards next to the edge of the board. Holding the board steady with the other hand slowly and carefully slide the knife towards you cutting along the outline.

Continue in the same way around the board, stopping and starting as necessary to reposition the board and keep the blade under control. Getting around the curves can be tricky at first, but as they say—practice makes perfect!

SETTING UP YOUR BOARD

Once you've gripped your board, use an Allen key to pierce the grip tape through the holes on the underside of your board. Then on the top of your board you can push the bolts into place.

Hold the bolts in place and turn your board over so you can attach the first truck.

The kingpin of your truck should always face inwards—towards the centre of your board.

When the truck is in place screw each of the nuts onto the bolts. You can easily do this by hand and then tighten them with a tool once the truck is on.

Use an Allen key on the top of your board, to hold the bolts in place, as you tighten each of the nuts at the back with a skate tool.
! BOARD TIP: Avoid over-tightening your deck bolts as this can cause your board to get stress cracks, which will weaken it.

Repeat the process with the other truck, and then you're ready to get your wheels on.

Each wheel will contain two bearings, which you can seat in your wheels using the axle of your truck. To do this drop the first bearing onto the axle.

Then grab your first wheel and, using the truck as leverage, push the wheel onto the bearing.

You'll know the bearing is seated properly when your wheel is right up against the hanger of the truck. Now remove this wheel from the axle so you can seat the second bearing.

Take your second bearing and put it on the axle. If you're using bearing spacers drop one of these onto the axle after the bearing. Still working on your first wheel, flip it over and press it down onto the bearing.

If you're using a spacer it should easily slide into the centre of your wheel, and the bearing should press in as usual.

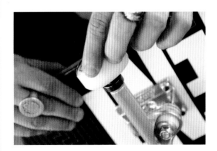

Repeat this process until all your wheels have bearings.

Now you're ready to screw all your wheels on.

Adding the washer before putting the nut on should stop the wheel nut from rubbing on the bearing.

Finally add the wheel nut.

Tighten the nut with a skate tool and repeat until all your wheels are on and you're ready to roll.

! WHEEL TIP: When tightening your wheel nuts be careful not to over-tighten as this will damage your bearings. Keep a small amount of play between your wheel nut and wheel to make sure it spins freely.

! BOARD TIP: Just as you wouldn't leave your board outside in the rain, avoid leaving it in really hot places like the car or in direct sunlight. These things can dry it out causing it to crack and warp.

SAFETY EQUIPMENT

When I was starting out I wore pads all the time and it helped me improve a lot quicker because I wasn't worried about hurting myself. I still wear pads whenever I'm trying a new trick in a bowl, or if I'm skating a vert ramp—it's a must. Even on a street course, wearing pads can make your progression much faster.

Unlike in Australia, lots of public skateparks around the world have compulsory helmet and pad rules. This isn't a bad thing; as I mentioned above it can help with confidence and, for your own safety, prevent painful injuries.

A friend of mine is a doctor and he also skates, so he's familiar with the risks of skateboarding. In most of the cases he treats related to skateboarding, the injury could have been prevented through the use of proper safety gear. In his experience the most skateboarding related injuries he sees are from beginner to intermediate level skaters. So when you see pro skaters doing crazy tricks in dvds and magazines, remember they've often spent years on their board to achieve that level of skill and proficiency!

HELMET
Helmets save lives. When you're purchasing a helmet, make sure it fits securely and is suitable for skateboarding.

KNEE PADS
Knee pads are great when you're learning, especially on transition, as you can bail out of tricks by sliding on your knees.

WRIST GUARDS
The natural instinct when falling is to put your arms out to stop yourself. Not only will wrist guards brace and protect your wrists, they'll also save your palms from bruising and skin loss.

ELBOW PADS
Check out any seasoned skateboarder's elbows and the scabs and scars will tell you that your elbows cop a beating when you slam. A good set of elbow pads will save you from the pain of impact and grazes.

Sequence: Andrew Peters

Backside 360
Five Dock, NSW

Photo: Steve Gourlay

LOCKING DOWN
THE BASICS
THE FUNDAMENTALS OF SKATEBOARDING

For most people, establishing their stance and basic skateboarding fundamentals like pushing and turning comes naturally, especially if you surf or play another sport where you need a certain amount of coordination. Even so, down the track when you're stuck scratching your head because you can't seem to land a trick, it often comes down to something as simple as fine-tuning the basics.

A classic example is if you find yourself pushing with your front foot, you could do yourself an instant favour and re-learn to push with your back foot. This will develop a stronger stance and enhance your balance so when you're approaching a trick you're better prepared and can focus on doing the manouevre rather than struggling to get there in the first place.

So much of skateboarding is about trial and error. If you put in the groundwork and spend plenty of time on your board your skill level will improve before you can say "Yeeeew!!!". Whether you feel like you need to go back to the drawing board or you're just starting out, this section might help get you there a little sooner.

STANCE }

Whether you're natural or goofy footed, a good stance enables you to be balanced and in control of your board.

REGULAR: LEFT FOOT FORWARD

GOOFY: RIGHT FOOT FORWARD

Goofy or natural, the specifics of a good stance are the same. Your front foot should be just behind the front bolts of your board and your back foot just behind the back bolts on the tail. You could think of your front foot as the "steering wheel" as this is the foot you put pressure on to turn your leading truck. Your back foot could be thought of as the "accelerator" as this will become your pushing foot and give you your speed.

Your body weight should feel centred and equally distributed through your legs and feet and onto the board.

A good stance includes having good flexibility through your knees and generally keeping them slightly bent. This will help with balance, turning and, down the track, *power*.

The first time I stepped on a skateboard, I naturally put my left foot forward and my right foot at the back. It just felt comfortable so I stuck with being natural footed. Since then a mate has also showed me a technique you can use to work it out—so if you're unsure you could give this a go.

Get a friend to stand behind you and give you a push to move you off your feet. When you're shoved you'll instinctively plant one of your feet out to stop yourself from falling over. The foot you put out is likely to be the front foot of your skateboarding stance. This test is by no means foolproof, although I have tried it

and I always put my left foot forward without even thinking about it.

However you work it out, the opposite of the stance you choose will become your "switch" stance. Lots of great skaters can skate both ways so if you want to shred like a pro it won't hurt to get familiar with rolling both ways.

PUSHING }

There are two methods of pushing: back foot pushing [normal] and front foot pushing [mongo]. A mongo push is a precarious and ugly way to get around, and should be avoided at all costs.

Starting off on flat, place your front foot on your board facing towards the nose and just behind the front deck bolts. Your back foot should be on the ground alongside your board.

Push off with your back foot, while keeping your weight through your front foot. Your back foot should remain connected with the ground while your board and body begin to roll forward.

Once your back leg is fully extended, it is time to lift it off the ground and put it on your board.

As your pushing foot comes back onto the board it's time to adjust your front foot position. Your toes should move from pointing towards the nose of your board to pointing to the side of your board. You'll now be in a regular cruising position.

From the cruise position, with your front foot just behind your front bolts and your back foot over your tail, you'll be ready to head into a turn, or set up for a trick.

A good solid pushing technique will go a long way to giving you a good all-round style.

TURNING }

This is where you learn to 'steer' your skateboard, so it's important your trucks are up for the challenge—make sure they're not too tight or you'll really struggle to change direction.

To get the hang of turning find a slight incline, rather than a flat surface. That way you can focus on the act of turning rather than propulsion. Once you're rolling, the first phase of the turn is to look in the direction you want to go.

Turn your head and then follow with your shoulder and so on down through your legs to the heels of your feet. In this case I'm turning to my left [frontside if you're regular footed] so my weight is on my heels.

If I wanted to turn right [backside] my weight would be on my toes. Simply put, whichever way you lean is the way you'll turn.

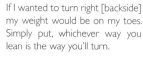  

Once you're turning, if you take your weight off your heels [or toes if you're turning backside] and balance your weight equally again on your board you'll continue rolling straight again.

To slow down, take long carves from side to side. To speed up, you can carve left to right, back and forth really quickly, and this motion will generate speed.

SLIDING }

The slide, AKA: four-wheel slide; AKA: cess slide is bucket-loads of fun, AND as skateboards don't have brakes, it's good to have some way to stop, right?

You can do these on flat ground, but if you find a spot with a slight incline and a smooth surface it will be much easier to learn. It will also help if you are travelling quite fast so you keep rolling after the slide, but do this within your limits.

Start off with your front foot just behind your front bolts, and your back foot slightly behind the back bolts. Your heels should hang just over the side of your board. Your knees should be bent, ready to start the slide.

Using your back foot, apply pressure to the heelside edge of your board and straighten your leg out to throw [push] the tail around into a slide.

As your board starts to come around, sit back on it a little and dig your heels in. Your front foot and back foot should now have equal pressure on the heelside edge of your board. During the slide your wheels should make a satisfying "brnnnnnt" or a "frnnnnnt" type of noise.

To take your board out of the slide and rolling forwards again, you simply have to relax and ease your weight off your back foot and you should automatically return to rolling normally.

All things going to plan and depending on the steepness of your chosen hill, you'll now be travelling slower than you were before the slide.

THE OLLIE }

The ollie is one of the most fundamental elements of skateboarding. Most of the tricks shown in this book incorporate an ollie in one way or another—so if there is one trick worthy of your time, patience and perseverance, this is it.

In the lead-up to the ollie your front foot should be positioned slightly behind your front bolts, with your back foot positioned on the end of the tail.

Your knees should be slightly bent and your back heel lifted up so you're almost on the toes of your back foot ready for the pop.

Press your back foot down on the tail so it smacks the ground. At the same time drag your front foot towards the nose of the board. The tap with the back foot and the upwards slide of the front foot happens very quickly, so timing is really important.

As your front foot drags toward the nose of the board, start to apply some pressure to the nose, and open the space between your knees slightly. This will help level the board out and keep you airborne for a fraction longer.

At this stage it's better to have the nose pointed down slightly [boned] than it is to have the tail end of the board pointing down [mob/rocket].

When you're landing, aim to have both feet flat on the board and positioned over your bolts. As you touch down keep your weight centred, bend your knees slightly to absorb the impact, and roll away.

Everyone has different preferences when it comes to the stance for ollies, so you should experiment with your foot positioning until you feel balanced and comfortable. A successful ollie will result from a combination of good foot positioning, weight distribution and timing.

BACKSIDE CARVE }

Carving is essentially the same technique as turning, but you're doing it on a curved wall 'transition' instead of on flat ground. This tip will be fundamental if you're wanting to skate a bowl or even the bowled areas of skateparks.

In the lead-up to the carve look at the transition and draw an imaginary arc on the wall, where you want to carve.

There are two tips to steal from the turning section that will help you to carve. Firstly, like you would on the flat, keep all four wheels on the transition during the turn. Secondly, to help you do this, make sure your trucks are loose enough so that they're responsive when you put weight either on your heels or toes.

As you reach the top of the carve maintain the pressure on your toe-side edge as you continue to travel around the arc. Spreading your arms out from your sides will counter-balance your upper body and help pull you around the curve.

As you come down the wall start straightening your legs as you ride through the transition. Coming down you'll naturally pick up speed, which can sometimes feel like you've been fired out of a slingshot. When you're learning you can start your carves lower in the bowl and then work your way up.

Roll into the transition with your feet balanced and in a comfortable cruising position. So you have enough momentum to get right around the 'arc' it's important at this point to really propel yourself up the wall. Then, keeping your knees bent, lean onto the toe-side edge of your board and begin to carve.

So much of skateboarding is about trial and error. If you put in the groundwork and spend plenty of time on your board your skill level will improve before you can say '*yeeeew!!!*'

CONDITIONS
AHEAD

Photo: Andrew Peters

Gap Ollie
Sydney, NSW

5 TRICKS TO LEARN WITHOUT LEAVING YOUR DRIVEWAY

NO SKATEPARK, NO WORRIES

Skating in your driveway is as classic as playing cricket in your backyard. I'm sure it's where lots of professional skateboarders started out, and where many more will. Even if you don't have a driveway, at the end of the day a flat piece of concrete is all you need.

Skateparks are great, but flat ground skating can be just as rewarding as skating a 12 foot bowl. All the time you put in, to learn tricks and challenge yourself, you'll get back triple in fun—right then and there and down the track. And … the best part is, you're in your own private training ground, with no crowds and no rules.

This section includes five essential flat ground tricks that you can learn within a stone's throw of your front door. Once you have these in the bag, the world is your oyster, and you can adapt them to any terrain you come across on your travels.

FRONTSIDE 180 OLLIE }

When you were learning regular ollies you probably found that you turned slightly frontside by accident. Given that you're familiar with the motion, you should now pick up proper frontside 180s, no sweat.

Roll at a speed that you are comfortable ollieing at, keeping in mind you're going to land this one rolling backwards.

Your upper body is as much a key to landing the frontside 180 ollie, as what your legs are to the ollie. Use your arms to 'wind up' your upper body—ie: swing your torso 90 degrees back towards the direction of your tail—as you smack your tail to the ground.

As you pop the tail, drag your front foot up the board as you would for an ollie. At the same time 'un-wind' your arms so they swing in the direction you want to turn. Your torso and legs should then follow.

Once you have dragged your foot to level out the ollie, dip the nose, and pull that tail around; the idea is to spin as much of the 180 in the air before you reconnect with the ground.

If you haven't turned the whole 180 you can sneak in a little nose drive on the front truck. To do this land with your weight above the nose and do a little pivot to get the whole way around. If you are opting for the more solid four-wheeled landing, spin the whole 180 degrees to land all four wheels at once.

As with any landing, crouch a little to absorb the impact, and maybe think of a trick to learn to get you back to rolling forwards. A switch frontside 180 or the half cab would be just the ticket.

BACKSIDE 180 OLLIE }

The backside 180 ollie is a truly classic trick that once you have down, will open the door to backside kickflips and heelflips and any backside tricks on ledges or rails.

Your torso should be facing almost completely forward at the start of the wind-up. As you tap your tail on the flat spin your upper body through the turn. The plan is that your board will follow the lead from your upper body.

On the flat I tend to scoop my 180s, so I'll guide you through this method. Rolling with your feet in the ollie position [but with your back foot a little more flattened] start to 'wind-up' your upper body. You're going to turn backside, so you should wind your body in the opposite direction.

As with most tricks on flat, you should be aiming to land centred. So, as you're coming back to the ground you will want both trucks should land at the same time. Unless, of course, you haven't quite spun the full 180, in which case a cheeky little 'nose drive' can be thrown in on the front truck. Although, for a decent sized 180 this isn't an option, so I wouldn't learn to rely on it.

So now you're rolling backwards, follow through with your head and make sure you're not about to run over a dog or another skater.

NOLLIE }

In theory any trick you can ollie into, you can nollie into too. So by getting your nollies down pat, you're essentially doubling the amount of tricks and combinations you can learn.

Once you're rolling, position your feet so that your front foot is on the front of the nose and your back foot somewhere in between the middle of the board and the back deck bolts.

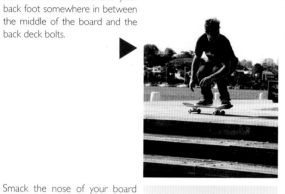

Bend your knees so that you are crouched down with your weight centred over the board. Just like the ollie, it will help if you are also slightly tip-toed in anticipation of the pop.

Smack the nose of your board into the ground and as it pops into the air drag your back foot back towards the tail in a smooth motion. As your foot reaches the tail, start levelling out your board out and focus on keeping both feet over the bolts.

Keep your board level and as you prepare to land, bend your knees slightly to absorb the impact.

Now stand-by for a whole new world of nollie madness.

SHOVE-IT }

Once you're happy with the pop on your ollie it's time to get ready for a Kung Fu lesson in the form of a crafty pop shove-it.

Take one big push-off to get you moving and then position your feet. Your front foot should be in the centre of the board just behind your front deck bolts and your back foot on your tail in an ollie position.

Once you're balanced begin to ollie but this time instead of your back foot just popping the tail, it should simultaneously pop and 'shove' your board behind you. This should cause your board to turn 180 degrees. Remember to keep your shoulders square, and face forward at all times.

As your board comes around have your front foot hovering ready for the catch. You want your leg in a slightly boned position to add that little bit of style.

Once your board hits your front foot, your back foot should be ready to stomp the board down for landing.

DON'T lean back on this trick; always stay on top of it for a smooth landing. Roll away and keep this one for your next line or as a warm-up in a game of S.K.A.T.E.

KICKFLIP }

In theory a kickflip is the same motion as an ollie with the addition of a flick of the front foot, so your board spins beneath you. You might want to master the ollie before trying this one.

Foot position is personal preference but the best place to start is to adopt a similar stance as you would for an ollie, only with your front foot slightly more to the heel-side of your board. Rolling at a comfortable speed, compress your knees and prepare to pop.

As your front foot drags towards the nose you want to give it a solid flick off the heel-side of the deck. This action is what will flip the board under your feet. It will take some trial and error to work out how much weight you have put behind the flick to complete a full rotation.

By now your board should be flipping underneath you. As you start coming back down to land, maintain the position of your legs and feet—you kind of have to trust that you will meet up with your board. Eye your board beneath you and get ready for the catch.

Ideally you should catch your board with your back foot over the back bolts and then bring your front foot on. Just like with the ollie, it would help with your landing to bone the nose down slightly. [And besides, it also looks more stylish than a flat or mob catch.]

Now the catch is complete it's just a matter of bending your knees to absorb the landing and rolling away.

Frontside Kickflip
Box Hill, VIC

FACING YOUR FEAR

In my experience people will scare themselves into not trying tricks—I know because I've done it before. Looking back on those moments, I've realised the fear factor only kicked in when I was facing a massive challenge. Eventually I'd face the challenge and overcome the fear, which would be a great feeling, and it's still one of the aspects of skateboarding I love the most.

Overcoming the fear isn't difficult—you just need to be physically and mentally on the same page, which really means you need to be confident mentally as well as physically competent. Confidence doesn't mean crazy —like trying to drop in before you can pump up the ramp and tailtap. Confidence comes through learning and perfecting tricks. Then you can apply what you know to tackle bigger and bigger challenges.

My first experience of real fear was dropping into a vert ramp. It was the first time I'd really encountered the thought "hey I could maybe hurt myself here". I was skating mainly parks and street at the time, but whenever I got a chance I would jump on the vert ramp and starting at the very bottom I'd practise pumping up the ramp, going higher and higher each time. Every now and then I'd walk up the stairs of the ramp and look down but I could never drop in. One day, it felt right so I put my board over the edge of the coping and

> " *If you* keep building your skills and confidence progressively, the fear factor, even though it might be there sometimes, becomes much *less noticeable.* "

dropped in. It didn't work out perfectly by any means but mentally it was a big step in facing my fear. I actually fell and landed at the bottom. I was fine because I had all my pads and helmet on but it shook me up for a few days. I kept skating as usual and built my confidence back up and the very next time I was at the ramp I went right back up there, dropped in and nailed it!! At that point it felt like the best day of my life.

Even now I still feel fear at times, when skating street more than anything, but I just accept the fear as a challenge and push myself bit by bit until I conquer it. The challenges are much bigger now but the feeling is the same and as good as that day at the ramp.

" *Get creative* and come up with new challenges for yourself, that way you'll already be thinking the way great skateboarders *think*. "

SHREDDING YOUR LOCAL

TRICKS AND TIPS FOR PARK SKATING

How good is it having a local park to shred? Especially when you're starting out, the repetition and practice on familiar terrain will definitely help you to learn tricks quicker.

If you're lucky your local park will have a range of various sized obstacles—whether it's transitions, ledges or rails—so you can keep stepping it up over time, taking the basics to the next level.

Don't be disheartened if you feel like your local park has nothing left to offer, but instead put in a bit of extra effort to get creative and come up with new challenges for yourself; that way you'll already be thinking the way great skateboarders think. And you never know, you might even inspire others around you to get amped, and fresh energy at the park is always a good thing.

As much as everyone loves their local, if you're up for a challenge [that word again] there's nothing better than mixing it up at another park and testing your skills on a whole new set of terrain. You'll know you've got tricks dialed if you can bust them anywhere.

Meanwhile, if you need inspiration for what to learn or do next, this section is dedicated to classic park skating.

Photo: Steve Gourlay

Backside Disaster
Cairns, QLD

DROPPING IN }

What the ollie is to flat ground, the drop-in is to ramps. Although scary at first, this trick is like riding a bike; do it once and you'll have it for the rest of your life.

Start off by putting your board over the ramp so your back trucks are sitting over the edge up against the coping. At this stage your back foot is holding down the tail and your front foot is just chilling on the platform.

Dropping in is about momentum, so you actually start dropping in as soon as you move your front foot off the platform to put it on your board. So the key to dropping in is to keep your front foot on the platform until you're completely ready to drop in.

When you're ready to drop in lift your front foot up and without hesitation place it onto the front of your board, lean forward and let the momentum take you.

Make sure you place your front foot just on or behind the front bolts and do it with confidence so you're essentially stomping your front wheels down into the transition.

Your instinct might tell you to lean back once you've stomped your board, but don't do it or chances are you'll whip out. Keep leaning forward as you roll down the ramp until you reach the flat. Then you can pull back, centre your weight again and roll away thinking about what to do next.

KICKTURN }

Rolling up the ramp is one thing—it's what you do to get back down again that is your ticket to good times: Enter the ever trusty kickturn.

When you're learning to kickturn, it doesn't matter whether you make the turn lower down the ramp, where the transition is mellow, or higher up. It's the technique you want to sort out first.

So when you're starting out, it will be easier if you approach the transition at a slight angle. Have your back foot positioned on the tail ready to apply pressure.

Once you're up the transition you can then execute the turn. You want it to be one smooth motion but to learn it you can think of it as three steps.

The first step is to apply pressure to your tail, so your front wheels lift off the ramp. [But don't lean backwards—keep your weight toward the direction you're travelling.]

The second step is to pivot on your back wheels so your body and board turn "sideways" to the ramp.

And then finally continue to pivot back down into the ramp.

Touch your front wheels down once you're facing back down into the ramp.

Keep on practising until you can do the kickturn in one smooth motion.

When you've really got your park skating dialed, you'll be pumping back down the transition as hard as you can to get up lots of speed to bust your next trick.

ROCK TO FAKIE }

An absolute classic park trick for all budding skateboarders to cut their transition teeth on. You'll have this nailed before your first drink break.

Make sure you have enough speed to reach the coping and roll up the transition with your nose squarely pointing at the coping. Avoid rolling up on an angle so your board doesn't slide out from underneath you.

As you reach the lip allow your front truck to lap over the coping and let the momentum carry the rest of your weight forward. You're aiming to end up somewhat on top of your board so you can "rock" it.

Once your front truck is clearly over the coping but your back truck is still hanging over the transition, "rock" your board by transferring weight to your front foot. Your front wheels should not quite touch the platform.

Then, like a see-saw, transfer the weight off your front foot and onto your back foot, so your board "rocks" back down into the transition. This should happen in one smooth motion.

The key to coming back in [ie to avoid hanging up] is to put enough pressure on your back foot to lift your front trucks up and out from the coping.

As soon as you get your front truck back over the coping, touch your front wheels down. Just as you began the trick, keep the nose of your board and your shoulders in a straight line, bend your knees into the transition and roll away.

BACKSIDE ROCK n ROLL }

This is a great trick with an even better name. It's the big brother to the backside kickturn and a must-have in any skater's repertoire.

Just as you would for a rock to fakie make sure you head up the transition with enough speed to reach the coping. It will also help if your front foot is a fraction back from your front bolts.

As you reach the lip allow your front truck to lap over the coping and let the momentum carry the rest of your weight forward. You're aiming to end up somewhat on top of your board so you can "rock" it [sound familiar?] and then "roll" it.

Now to execute the rock n roll. Straighten your front leg and push your front wheels down towards the platform. You want your back wheels to come right up to the coping. As you do this, turn your head and start bringing your shoulders around to face back into the ramp.

Continue to rotate your head and shoulders, shifting your weight back onto your back foot as you "rock" back into the ramp. As soon as this happens pivot on your back wheels so that you swing your board back into the ramp facing forward.

Once you've completed the rotation, re-adjust your weight so it is evenly spread over both feet, lean forward and roll away.

BACKSIDE BOARDSLIDE }

Boardslides will test your ollie and balance so it's a good feeling once you start nailing them. You can boardslide a curb, flat bar or ledge and—once you're feeling gnarly—you can step it up to handrails.

Take a couple of decent pushes and approach the rail at a slight angle, so that you are almost rolling parallel with it.

Spot the point on the rail where you want to start your slide and crouch down ready to ollie your board up and onto the rail.

As you pop your ollie you need to turn your board 90 degrees, so the rail is centred under your board.

As your board makes contact with the rail it's important to lean forward and keep your shoulders parallel with your board. This helps to keep the forward momentum of the slide. Leaning back too far will result in your board shooting out from underneath you—the result being your voice might become a few octaves higher.

Now it's time to find your balance and enjoy the slide. Without even thinking about it you'll probably find you put your arms out to balance, which is perfect.

As you approach the end of the rail, swing your shoulders around and put a little more weight on your back foot to help you pivot off the rail 90 degrees. As you pop off the rail, keep leaning forward and bend your knees to absorb the landing.

FRONTSIDE BOARDSLIDE }

Front boards can be challenging to learn, as you tend to get thrown onto your backside, but dust yourself off and keep trying because the end result has styles for miles.

I can't stress enough how important it is to be travelling at a good pace before jumping onto the rail. It may seem strange at first but a few slow attempts and seeing how your board stops dead in its tracks will convince you to put some extra gusto into your approach.

Approach facing the rail until you're rolling alongside it almost parallel.

As you ollie 90 degrees onto the rail, keep your shoulders and upper body parallel with the rail [you can see this well in the frame below].

As you begin to slide keep facing forward [the direction you are travelling], keeping your eyes on the landing point.

As long as your weight is centred [equally balanced on the nose and tail] you should find your board will centre itself over the rail, and you'll be sliding with success.

Now it's time to pop out. As you approach the end of the rail, put slightly more weight on the tail and pop out 90 degrees.

You should now find yourself rolling away forward from one of the most classic tricks of all time.

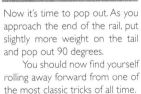

FRONTSIDE 50-50 GRIND }

Once you've mastered the ollie it's only a matter of time until you'll want to combine it into another trick and there is no better place to start than the frontside 50-50.

As with any grinding trick there's going to be a fair amount of friction between your trucks and the surface of the ledge you're planning to grind. So it is important to have plenty of speed to counteract this.

Approach the ledge at a slight angle and prepare to ollie to just above the height of the top of the ledge.

Concentrate on smacking your back truck down a fraction of a second before your front one. This will help to get the grind started without the front truck acting as a brake and pitching you forward.

As you lock into the 50-50 position and begin to grind, keep your weight over the toe-edge of your board. This will help keep you locked into position and prolong the length of your grind. Another thing that can help you to grind longer is keeping your weight slightly over your back foot.

As you prepare to pop out of the grind lift your front wheels up slightly and use your existing momentum to pop out. If the ledge doesn't have an end [as shown here] apply this same technique but this time ollie out at a slight angle and roll away.

FRONTSIDE TAILSLIDE }

Some people overlook the frontside tailslide because they think it's "kinda hard"—hopefully, with a bit of inside knowledge, you'll bust that myth once and for all.

Before you try this one it would help to learn frontside 180 ollies to tail on a curb or ledge. You also want to have your frontside grinds locked down, then you're good to go.

Travel up the transition with the same speed and angle as you would if you were going for a frontside grind.

When you're about a foot below the coping, lift your front wheels up and scoop the tail around as you would a frontside 180 ollie on the flat. Focus on the section of coping you want your tail to land on.

As the tail locks in to position transfer the majority of your weight onto your back foot and push it in the direction of the slide. Once you begin sliding, loosen up a little and let it rip.

As you feel the momentum of the slide start to ease up, lean forward slightly and turn your shoulders so that you are facing back into the ramp. You should head back down the transition as you would for a standard drop-in.

Keeping your weight forward, touch down with your front wheels, bend your knees slightly and roll away.

SKATEPARK ETIQUETTE

A crowded skatepark can be overwhelming when you're starting out and as far as I'm aware there are no written rules on skatepark etiquette. This is probably because it comes down to individuals using their own common sense. Making sure you're aware of your surroundings and respecting other skatepark users will go a long way to making your skatepark experience a good one.

HERE ARE A FEW GUIDELINES TO HELP YOU OUT.

BE AWARE OF YOUR SURROUNDINGS: Before you try a trick have a good look around and make sure there is no one else travelling in the direction of the area you want to skate.

WAIT YOUR TURN: At first it might look chaotic, but if you watch a session for a few minutes you'll notice that people do take it in turns. Avoid cutting in; no one likes a snake.

RESPECT THE LOCALS: To most locals the skatepark is their second home. Give them right of way, and in turn this respect should be reciprocated.

DON'T SIT ON LEDGES OR OTHER OBSTACLES: Most parks have seating provided, so avoid parking your butt on obstacles that other people might want to skate. If there aren't any seats, use your board.

CLEAN UP YOUR RUBBISH: Once again it comes down to respect—make sure you bin your trash or take it with you before leaving the park.

THINK TWICE BEFORE ACTING LIKE A GOOSE: Sure, you might be having a good time, but try to keep it chill. Throwing your board around if you can't land something probably isn't a good idea.

LOOK OUT FOR BMXers: The problem with sharing a park with bike riders is that you can't hear them coming. Nine times out of ten if a skater runs into a BMXer it's the skater comes off second best.

DON'T GET IN THE WAY: If you want to skate a flat section of the park, make sure it isn't a major thoroughfare or a section where other people want to session a particular obstacle.

APOLOGISE AND MOVE ON: Collisions do happen and in most cases neither party gets seriously hurt. If you are involved in a collision make sure the other person is okay, apologise and get back to skating.

OFFER A HAND: If someone has taken a slam, don't stand around like a goober; ask if they are okay and offer to help or get help if they are hurt.

SKATING A RAMP OR BOWL: If you bail or fall off that's your go done. Step off to the side and wait for your turn to come around again.

DON'T BE SCARED TO ASK FOR ADVICE: In most cases older skaters will be all too happy to offer advice if you ask for it.

Skateparks are built for everyone to use and as long as you bring a positive attitude you're bound to have a good time.

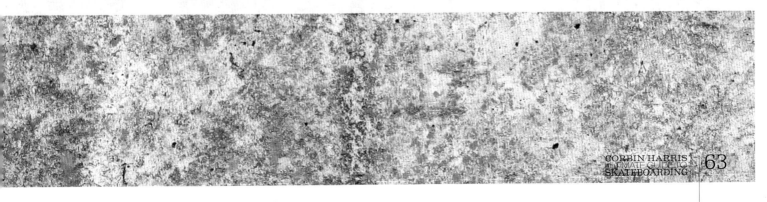

MANUAL }

At some point manuals used to be called wheelies, which is probably a better description since it is essentially the act of balancing on your back wheels.

Before giving this one a go, make sure you can ollie comfortably up a curb. It won't hurt to practise manuals on the flat before taking them to a manual pad. [If you're still working on ollies you can skip ahead a few frames to the actual manual.]

Approach the manual pad with more than enough speed to allow you to roll its entire length.

Where you normally level out the ollie, keep this one a little rocket or mob—landing with your tail angled towards the ground [see ollie]—so you land in the manual position.

As you reach the exit point keep your weight over your back trucks and tip your shoulders forward. Execute a lazy little ollie motion to pop you off the end of the pad.

When you're about a foot away from the manual pad, pop your ollie, keeping your eyes on the point where you want to land.

Locking in means finding the right balance between your front and back foot with your body weight centred in between. Think of your back truck like the middle of a see-saw and your feet are at either end—both feet are putting downwards pressure but are counter-balancing so neither end touches the ground.

Once you've found the sweet spot of balancing your manual enjoy the sensation of rolling on two wheels.

Spot the ground and aim to land solidly with all four wheels at once. Absorb the landing by bending your knees slightly and roll away.

FRONTSIDE GRIND }

If there is one trick you can do anywhere, anytime, on anything and it will always feel amazing, this is it.

Before getting started on this one make sure you're confident doing frontside kickturns. Approach the transition with double the speed you would for a kickturn, as this will help you reach the lip with enough momentum to grind once your truck makes contact with the coping.

Roll up the wall at approximately 45 degrees and just below the coping start to lift your wheels. Continue to propel yourself forward—if you lean back at this point you'll struggle to make it onto the coping.

When your outside wheel rolls over the coping and you feel the metal on metal, start to stand up slightly so you're almost upright over the coping. [Don't worry if you're not upright when you're starting out.] As you do this, transfer your weight to your back truck while counter-balancing the front truck [like a manual] and hold for as long as you can.

As you start slowing down, turn your head to look over your front shoulder—this will swing your upper body in the same direction.

Then follow through with your lower body so your trucks turn on the coping. Now you push down on the front of your board to re-enter the bowl—just like you would dropping in.

When you feel all four wheels make contact with the surface of the transition, lean forward, compress your knees and roll away.

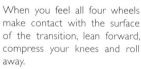

HEELFLIP TO FAKIE }

Do yourself a favour and learn heelflips on flat ground before taking them to a bank or transition. You'll then have them dialed in no time!

You should roll straight up the transition with enough speed as if you were to do a lofty ollie to fakie. Your feet should be in a heelflip position; front foot well behind the bolts with your toes hanging over the edge, back foot ready for the pop, with your toes centred on the tail.

You should aim to tap your tail as late as possible, in fact, just before your front wheels hit the coping. As you pop off your tail, slide your front foot upwards so your heel flicks up and off of the toe-side of your board.

In one fluid motion, when you're popping your tail and flicking your front foot, your legs are also sucking up under you at the same time. Your board should then flip beneath you while you prepare for the catch that awaits.

You should aim to catch your board with your back foot first and as this happens, you should be at the peak of your trick.

When you are reunited with your board, decompress your legs and stomp your board down into the transition—landing both sets of wheels at once.

When you're up for the challenge move onto steeper or higher transitions.

FEEBLE GRIND }

You could almost think of a feeble grind as a cross between a boardslide and a backside 5-0. It's also similar to a smith grind except in a feeble your front truck is above the coping or rail instead of below.

Approach the bar backside on a slight angle and get ready to ollie. As you pop, snap and drag your ollie, you will barely have to change your direction, as the angle of the feeble is similar to the angle that you have approached it on.

Clear the bar with your front truck, as if you were going to do a boardslide, but don't turn. Instead, keep your current angle and engage the back truck with the rail. It might help if you get your legs into a feeble position in the air. This consists of an outstretched, boned front leg, and a slightly tucked back leg.

As you engage, or even just before, transfer your weight to your back leg. This will apply pressure to your back trucks, which in combination with the forward position of your boned front leg, will keep the grind going.

As you reach the end of the rail keep the weight on your back foot and slightly lift up the nose of your board so you pop off and roll away.

360 FLIP TO FAKIE }

AKA: tre flip, is a great looking trick, and if you're worried you can't even do them that well on the flat, don't despair as they're easier on a flat bank than you may think.

Try a 360 flip to fakie on a flat bank that you can comfortably ollie fakie on. You should roll up the bank with your feet in the tre flip position: front foot behind your bolts, angled slightly towards the nose and with your heel hanging off the side; back foot with the toes on the toe-side corner of the tail.

Just before you stop and roll back down the bank, execute the flip. You should pop the tail and shove the board 360 with your back foot, and at the same time flip your board with your front foot. Your front foot should flick up and off the nose.

At this point your feet should separate in a scissor fashion: your front leg should extend forward and straighten, while the back foot should get tucked up under your rear.

You should try to catch your board with your outstretched front leg, just as it finishes the flip and the 360 rotation.

It is almost as if you pass the board from your back foot [before popping] to your front foot [for catching].

Your back foot should reconnect with your board after your front foot and just before landing. Stomp that puppy and roll away.

BACKSIDE GRIND }

When it comes to skating transition, nothing beats the sensation of grinding. Once you're comfortable kickturning frontside and backside you're ready to get crazy and hit the lip!

As you approach the quarter pipe, your feet should be positioned similar to if you were dropping in—with your back foot square across the tail and your front foot approximately over your front bolts. It's also important to make sure you have enough speed to reach the coping.

As you travel up the wall bend your knees slightly and begin the motion of a backside carve, focusing your eyes on the section of coping you want your back truck to make contact with.

As you reach the peak of your turn, transfer your weight to the tail ready for the back truck to start grinding.

Once you're over the coping shift your body weight directly over the top of the board while making sure to keep that front truck lifted. Enjoy that grind.

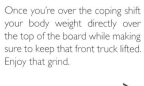

When you feel the sensation of the grind slowing down it's time to transfer your weight back into the ramp. I find it helps if you think about letting your leading shoulder guide you in. With your knees slightly bent continue down the wall and roll away.

Backside Grind

SKATE PARK GLOSSARY

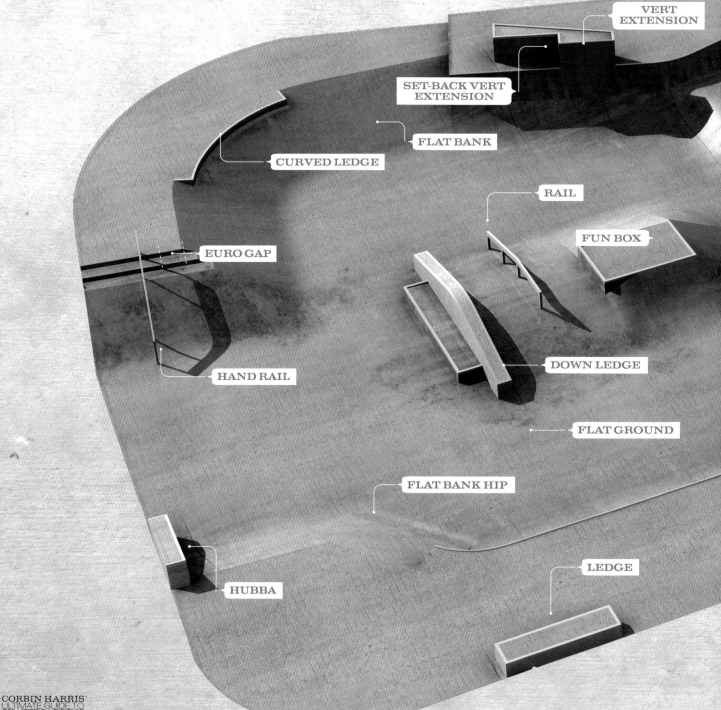

VERT EXTENSION

SET-BACK VERT EXTENSION

FLAT BANK

CURVED LEDGE

RAIL

FUN BOX

EURO GAP

DOWN LEDGE

HAND RAIL

FLAT GROUND

FLAT BANK HIP

HUBBA

LEDGE

Park design: Convic

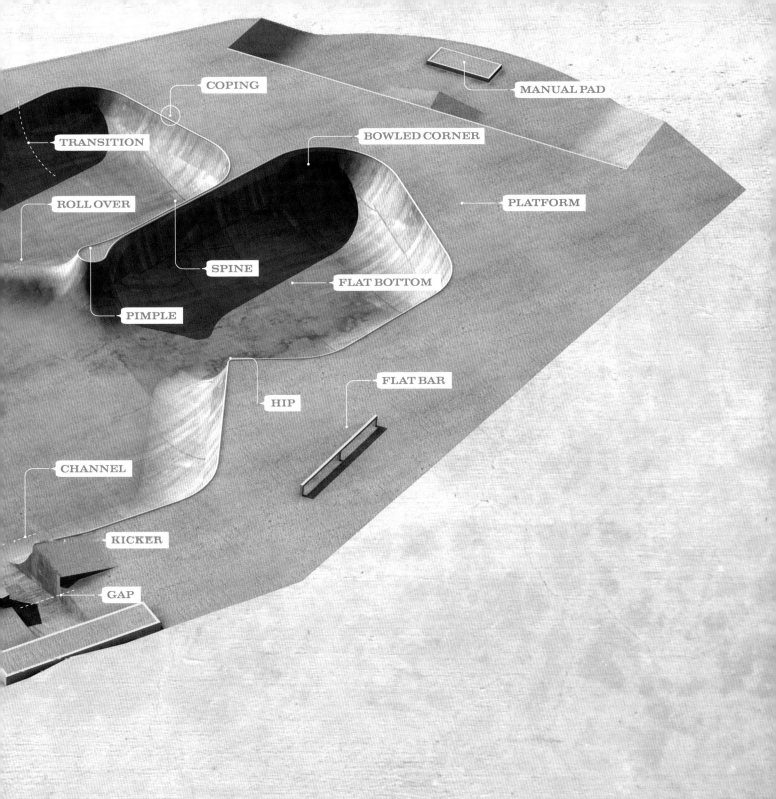

COPING

TRANSITION

BOWLED CORNER

MANUAL PAD

ROLL OVER

PLATFORM

SPINE

FLAT BOTTOM

PIMPLE

HIP

FLAT BAR

CHANNEL

KICKER

GAP

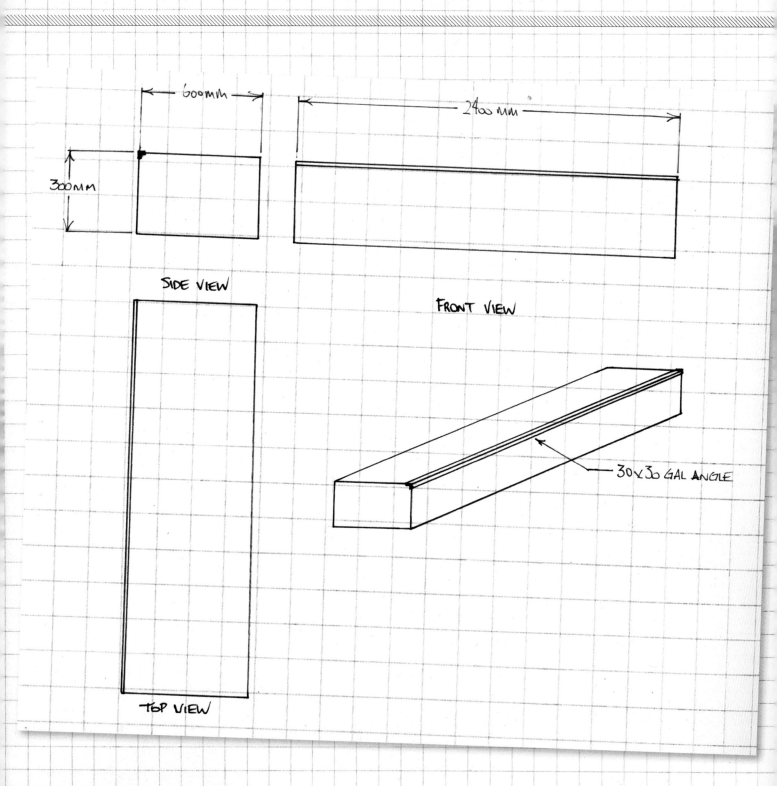

600mm

300MM

SIDE VIEW

2400 MM

FRONT VIEW

TOP VIEW

30 x 30 GAL ANGLE

HOW TO BUILD A LEDGE

Try this out for size for a weekend project—by that I mean build it on Saturday morning and spend the rest of the weekend skating it. Okay, so I had some help from my mates, but who wouldn't; in addition to materials and tools you need someone who knows what they're doing!

Take this list down to your local hardware supplier, and if they're good dudes they'll cut everything to size for you—that way you get to keep your hands and eliminate the need for a hand saw or circular saw. Then all you need to worry about is drilling and screwing all the pieces together.

SPECIFICATIONS: Ledge/manual pad 2400mm (long) x 600mm (wide) x 300mm (high)

MATERIALS REQUIRED:

70mm x 35mm Pine [for framework]
2 x 2400mm lengths
4 x 1095mm lengths
6 x 230mm lengths
10 x 570mm lengths

12mm CD grade Plywood [for top and sides]
1 x 600mm (w) x 2400mm (l) sheet
2 x 300mm (w) x 2400mm (l) sheets

30mm x 30mm Galv angle steel [for edging]
1 x 2400mm length

Hardware
approx 100 65mm x 8 gauge tek screws
approx 50 25mm x 8 gauge tek screws

TOOLS NEEDED:

Battery drill + 3mm and 10mm drill bits for metal and #2 phillips bit for screws
Hand saw or circular saw [only if you can't get your materials pre-cut]
Square
Hammer
Tape measure / pencil

1. If your ply is pre-cut you should have three pieces as shown here for the sides and top of the ledge. If you're starting with one sheet of ply and you need to cut the pieces, measure your widths starting from one corner and work your way down. Mark it out at both ends so you can match up the marks and rule a straight cutting line across the ply.

When you're cutting, make sure you're working on a steady surface, and get someone to hold the timber securely while you cut. Take care especially if you're using power tools, or get someone else to cut the timber for you.

2. You can now start laying out your framework. Using 6 x 570mm lengths and 6 x 230mm lengths lay out the three box sections ready for assembly. You should have left over 4 x 570mm lengths, 2 x 2400mm lengths and 4 x 1095mm lengths, which you can put aside for use later on.

3. To assemble the box sections of the framework, it is important to mark out and pre-drill the screw holes. These 'pilot holes' will make it easier to drill the screws in, and stop the timber from splitting.

4. Now screw each of the box frames together with the 65mm tek screws, going through the pilot holes until the screws sit flush with the timber.

5. Now you can stand your three box frames on their sides and run the 2 x 2400mm lengths of pine through the bottom of the frames. Attach these by marking out and pre-drilling through the outside of the frame and then screwing the 65mm screws through the pilot hole.

6. Now you can attach the two plywood sides. You'll see one was done in the previous step. Using the 25mm tek screws, attach the plywood to each of the three box frames. You'll only need to use six screws on each side for now, as there is still more framing to come which will make it more secure.

7. Once the sides are attached, locate the 4 x 1095mm lengths of timber as these will now be incorporated into the frame. Run each of these lengths in between each of the original box frames and screw to the plywood using the 25mm tek screws.

8. You should now only have 4 x 570mm lengths of timber and the plywood top to attach. The four timber lengths form the battens, as you can see above, that will help structurally complete the ledge and provide support for the top. Use your hammer to tap each length into position between the original box frames. Check that they're square before screwing them to the sides. You'll need to use 65mm tek screws.

9. Here's an important tip before you attach the ply top: make sure you have the frame sitting on a nice flat level surface; if you don't you will find it will be out of square. So speaking of square, grab your square and make sure everything is looking tight; also measure from opposite corner to corner to make sure it's square lengthways. Lay the 12mm ply on top and fix down to all the battens with the 25mm tek screws.

10. Now you're ready to attach the metal edging. First lay the metal angle along the edge of the ledge and mark out where all the battens are so you know where the screws will be going. Using a 3mm drill bit (for metal) drill your pilot holes. Then using a 10mm drill bit (for metal) carefully drill through each pilot hole, just only a couple of mm into the metal. This will allow you to countersink the screws.

11. To screw down the edging, hold it tightly in position and use the 65mm tek screws to fix it down. Because you've pre-drilled a shallow hole with the 10mm drill bit, your screws should sit just flush or slightly below the surface of the metal.

12. If your materials were cut to length, you shouldn't have any overhang with the metal edging and if anything you could just smooth off the edge with a metal file. If there is any overhang you'll need to get someone to cut it off with a hack saw or angle grinder, and again make sure the end is filed smooth.

13. You should now have a completed ledge! At some point when it's not in use, maybe consider giving it a coat of paint, which will help to protect it from the elements. Now turn back a few pages to brush up on your grinds then you're ready to roll.

Photo: Andrew Peters

Crooked Grind
Sydney, NSW

CORBIN HARRIS'
ULTIMATE GUIDE TO
SKATEBOARDING

TICKET TO RIDE

One of the best things about skateboarding professionally, other than actually skating, is it allows me to travel. Whether I'm travelling within Australia or overseas, going to familiar places or places I've never been, there is still a buzz about a change of scene and the prospect of discovering something new. It's especially insane experiencing new cultures and skating new things—both these things can be a challenge, which I think can bring out the best in people and help them evolve. Myself included.

Most of the time I'm travelling with one of my sponsors' teams, and we'll have a filmer and photographer with us and be aiming to shoot some good coverage of everyone in the team. Even though skateboarding is an individual sport, when you're travelling with a team you definitely have to be a team player so that everyone comes home with some tricks captured on film.

The types of trips vary from being flown to New York and staying in good hotels to camping, road trips and BBQs. Either kind of trip is just as important and just as fun as the other. Like on a road trip in New Zealand a few years back, we were driving all night in between locations and eventually pulled over to camp for the night. It felt like we were in the middle of nowhere, but when we woke up in the morning

> *Whether* I'm travelling within Australia or overseas, there is still a buzz about a change of scene and the prospect of discovering *something new*.

there was the beautiful ocean on one side with lots of noisy seals, and amazing snow capped mountains on the other. Days on the road are perfect because you never really know what you're going to get.

Lots of a skateboarders' life is spent travelling, so it helps if you enjoy it. I find that I've now got friends who are like extended family all around the world, and although we might not see each other often, it's always just as cool when we do catch up. As much as I love travelling, it's a cliché but it's true, it makes me appreciate all the good things about being at home even more.

Backside Smith Grind
Cairns, QLD

10
SKATEPARKS
YOU HAVE TO
SKATE

Australia has some of the best public skateboarding facilities in the world. If I have to travel for hours to check out a park, I don't think twice, even if it means jumping on a plane—but, more and more, great parks are popping up on my doorstep.

What's even better is that the design and construction is improving with each new breed of skatepark, so no matter where you are in Australia you're guaranteed access to some quality terrain.

CAIRNS
SKATEPARK
QUEENSLAND

Located right next to the ocean, this has to be one of the most scenic, not to mention expansive, skateparks in Australia.

The plaza-style street area consists of all varieties of banks, stairs, rails and blocks and is so amazingly landscaped it's easy to forget you're still in a skatepark and not on the street.

The bowl section is huge and includes various sized capsules for all levels of skater. The cradle is one of the main features of the big bowl and is nothing to be scared of as you can cruise through it without having to go upside down. The tombstone in the bowl is definitely my favourite section of the park, although it's impossible to get sick of cruising the plaza.

This is one of those rare parks you could stay at for the whole day or weekend and never get sick of the place. What makes it even better are the BBQs within the area and a nearby free-of-charge swimming pool to cool off from that crazy North Queensland heat!!

All photos: Convic

FAST FACTS

ADDRESS: The Esplanade, Cairns

YEAR COMPLETED: 2006

NO. SQUARE METRES: 3080m²

LIGHTS AT NIGHT: YES

CROCODILES: YES

AVERAGE TEMPERATURE: 29 degrees C

HOURS TO GREAT BARRIER REEF: 1.5 hrs by boat

Frontside Pivot to Fakie
Cairns, QLD

ADELAIDE SKATEPARK

SOUTH AUSTRALIA

The best thing about this park is the fact that it is slap bang in the middle of the city—close to shops, public transport and hotels.

Considering its central location, this place is enormous and has a huge range of transition and street obstacles, allowing you to link up lines all over the place.

The array of legit street-style rails and hubbas range in size from the likes of intermediate 3-stairs to heavy duty 10-stairs. The capsule bowl section with its spine, hips and extensions is a little challenging but always good fun.

There's generally plenty of room for everyone here, but throw more than a few bikers in the mix and things tend to get a little hectic on the collision front.

The variety of terrain makes this place a breeding ground for good all-round skateboarders. If this sounds like you, you'll love this place. If this doesn't sound like you, you'll love it anyway, because whatever you're into—it's here!

All photos: Steve Gourlay

FAST FACTS

ADDRESS: NORTH TERRACE, ADELAIDE CITY

YEAR COMPLETED: 2000

LIGHTS AT NIGHT: YES

DISTANCE TO BEACH: 7kms

WHITE POINTERS: YES

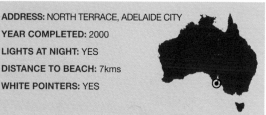

Photo: Steve Gourlay

Photo: Convic

Photo: Brett Jordan

FRANKSTON SKATEPARK

VICTORIA

One of the biggest and best skateparks in Victoria, Frankston has it covered with a massive street course as well as two different types of bowl.

The street course includes everything you would expect—flat bars, ledges, flat bank hips and wallrides, which flow into a bigger section with waist-high hand-rails and hubba-style ledges. The whole place is so spread out with plenty of flat ground, giving you time to hit all the different obstacles while stringing together lines from one end of the park to the other.

The smaller bowl is a perfect size for anyone starting out, or for the confident skater to warm up before getting gnarly. You can skate it like a mini ramp (back and forth) or carve it like a bowl.

The "big" bowl is more of a commitment being 13 foot in the deep end, and features pool coping, a death box and tiles for a legit pool sensation.

The local Frankston skaters are pretty lucky to have such an amazing skatepark at their disposal.

FAST FACTS

ADDRESS: CRANBOURNE RESERVE, SAMUEL SHERLOCK ROAD, FRANKSTON

YEAR COMPLETED: 2006

NO. SQUARE METRES: 2070m²

HOURS FROM MELBOURNE: < 1 hr

POOL COPING: YES

ONSITE CANTEEN: YES

EAGLEHAWK SKATEPARK

BENDIGO, VICTORIA

This concrete playground is one of the best all-round parks in Australia, with such a variety of obstacles you can try just about anything.

The street course, including rails, blocks, ledges and flatbanks, leads into a small spine with some other street-like banks. In this part of the park my favourite spot would have to be the euro step-up gap, which is easy to get up even for beginners. If you've learnt a flip trick on the flat you could easily step it up and take it to this obstacle.

Obviously I love the bowl section with its decent size transitions, including an over-vert section to keep the crazier crew on their toes. Its clean concrete finish makes it much safer to bail tricks and slide out of them without losing too much skin.

The best thing about parks with this much space is that even when a session is crowded there is still room for everyone to have a good time.

FAST FACTS

ADDRESS: CANTERBURY PARK, EAGLEHAWK, BENDIGO

YEAR COMPLETED: 2008

NO. SQUARE METRES: 1185m²

HOURS FROM MELBOURNE: 2.5hrs

POOL COPING: YES

KANGAROOS: YES

Backside Lipslide
Eaglehawk, VIC

WATERLOO SKATEPARK

SYDNEY, NSW

Considering the small amount of space the designers had to work with, they did a really good job of making this a functional and fun park.

Predominantly a plaza-style design, this place is loaded with a variety of ledges, rails, manual pads and banks. On the street course itself there are no real transitions to speak of but this is one of the factors that makes the place way more interesting to skate than your standard park.

If you're feeling like dropping hammers, there's a legitimate sized handrail and hubba ledge, but if mellowness is your game the place is great for cruising and carving the assorted banks.

On any given day you'll see numerous heated battles of S.K.A.T.E. on the ample flatland but it's the ledges that always see the majority of punishment. There is also a 3 foot metal mini ramp that was cut down from the "sort of" vert ramp that sat at the original park over a decade ago.

Local skaters and visiting pros alike use 'Ferny' as a warm-up spot before going out and handling more serious business.

Just be careful, though—this place is so much fun your warm-up might see you getting stuck here all day.

All photos: Steve Gourlay

FAST FACTS

ADDRESS: WATERLOO OVAL, ELIZABETH STREET (CNR MCEVOY ST)

YEAR COMPLETED: 2006

AKA: FERNSIDE

DISTANCE FROM CITY CENTRE: 2.5kms

LIGHTS AT NIGHT: YES

CHIMA: YES

Photo: Steve Gourlay

Photo: Steve Gourlay

Photo: Pete Daly

BONDI
SKATEPARK

SYDNEY, NSW

Set right in the middle of iconic Bondi Beach I'm surprised this skatepark doesn't have its own reality TV show.

Filled with transitions, it includes a big swimming pool-like bowl as well as a smaller street course area. The bowl is the main attraction here, with its sheer size, perfect coping and pool tiles. The street course is tough to skate if there are more than a few people skating at the same time, but can still provide you with a great session and there is nothing better than flying around it as fast as you can.

It can get really packed here from 3pm on weekdays until sundown, so if you're not up for a crowd, come earlier in the day. On the weekends it gets pretty crowded on both days and there's usually no less than 50 tourists standing around the bowl watching the action.

The location alone ensures this place always has a good vibe.

FAST FACTS

ADDRESS: ELIZABETH DRIVE, BONDI BEACH

YEAR COMPLETED: 2004

BOWL DEEP END: 11 foot

DISTANCE FROM SYDNEY CITY: 7kms

POOL COPING: YES

TOPLESS SUNBATHERS: YES

Frontside Air
Victoria Park, WA

Photo: Luke Thompson

Photo: Steve Gourlay

Photo: Luke Thompson

VICTORIA SKATEPARK

PERTH, WA

The folks in Perth are lucky enough to have one of the smoothest bowls in Australia. This place features a tiled deep end with one of the biggest "death boxes" I've seen in Australia—even basic tricks done over this are a major achievement.

The deep end connects with a smaller bowl, which has an amazing hip for blasting airs and generating too much speed for the other end of the bowl. Yep, I said too much speed, as this corner whips you around so fast you can find yourself blasting head-height airs before you know it.

Vic bowl is the perfect mix of large and small sections making it perfect for seasoned old bowl dogs and beginners alike.

As with many of Perth's skateparks, this is set alongside the water, so it's got a very mellow vibe. Any time I'm lucky enough to find myself in Western Australia, this is always one of the first places I head to.

FAST FACTS

ADDRESS: VICTORIA PARK, CANNING HWY

YEAR COMPLETED: 2007

DISTANCE FROM PERTH: 5kms

DEEP END: 9 foot

SHALOW END: 6 foot

POOL COPING: YES

BLACK SWANS: YES

FIVE DOCK SKATEPARK
SYDNEY, NSW

This would have to be one of the biggest bowls in Australia, comprising three different sections. The first section includes the original and iconic Five Dock bowl [circa early 80s], which, as well as the old snake-run, has been incorporated into the new design. The two new sections are an intermediate and big bowl, which includes an over-vert taco, a spine, channels, pimples and, between them all, multiple combinations of hips and potential transfer combos.

Ever since this place was built, it has reminded me of the concrete bowls you find in Europe, with most of the walls 6 foot plus. The new bowl section is by far my favourite part of this park, and with plenty of speed the most basic tricks feel awesome.

The only downside is that ful-tilt street skaters may find their attention span drift away here, but the upside is that this park is absolute heaven for anyone who loves going fast on a skateboard.

All photos: Steve Gourlay

FAST FACTS

ADDRESS: FIVE DOCK RESERVE, INGHAM AVENUE, SYDNEY

YEAR COMPLETED: 2007

POOL COPING: YES

KOOKABURRAS: YES

NO. OF DOCKS: 5

NERANG SKATEPARK

GOLD COAST, QLD

All photos: Rome Torti

Nerang is a large and well thought out skatepark in that it combines street and transition really well. Over half of the park is street oriented, with a circuit-style course that includes flat bars, ledges, hubbas, euro gaps and flat bank hips. The street area flows into a bowled section which features a spine, an over-vert section and even a doorway channel set into the biggest wall. There is also a super fun-sized kidney bowl with pool coping.

This is another park that's great for learning and warming up before taking your tricks to bigger terrain.

The spread-out design also allows large crowds to session the place without it ever feeling too crowded.

If parks of this standard keep being built in Australia it's only a matter of time until more great pro skaters come out of this country.

FAST FACTS

ADDRESS: ARTHUR EARLE PARK, NERANG CONNECTION ROAD

YEAR COMPLETED: 2009

DRIVE FROM GOLD COAST: 30 mins

POOL COPING: YES

CANE TOADS: YES

Backside Tailslide
West Hobart, TAS

Photo: Jason Morey

Photo: Steve Gourlay

Photo: Jason Morey

WEST HOBART SKATEPARK

TASMANIA

To me this is what skateboarding is all about—awesome locals, raw terrain and a relaxed atmosphere.

West Hobart bowl was built 30 odd years ago and its rough, aged surface makes for skateboarding at its rawest. It comprises of a huge snake-run about 150 metres long, which starts off at about 1 foot deep and eventually winds its way into a kinked 10 foot bowl.

Awww yeah!!! I get excited just thinking about this place. Depending on your mood you can mess around in the shallow sections, do full speed snake runs all day, or step up to the deep end. The constant uphill journey back up to the start of the snake-run is more than enough incentive for you to make sure you land your tricks.

While not for the faint hearted the West Hobart bowl is worth the airfare to Tasmania alone. Even if this kind of place isn't your thing, I challenge any skater to not be amazed by the sheer sight of this concrete dinosaur.

As you can see from the pictures, there's barely a perfect transition in the place, but that's one of the best things about it. Tassie is an amazing place and one of my top 10 destinations in the world.

FAST FACTS

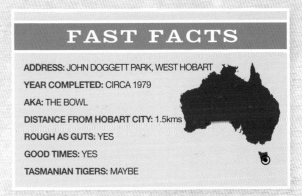

ADDRESS: JOHN DOGGETT PARK, WEST HOBART

YEAR COMPLETED: CIRCA 1979

AKA: THE BOWL

DISTANCE FROM HOBART CITY: 1.5kms

ROUGH AS GUTS: YES

GOOD TIMES: YES

TASMANIAN TIGERS: MAYBE

Photo: Steve Gourlay

Kickflip to Fakie
Tasmania

Corbin, Jake Duncombe and Dustin Dollin

MATES

INSPIRATION CLOSE TO HOME

So many good skateboarders have come out of Australia over the years. The one thing all these people have in common is the passion to do what they love and that's what gets me inspired. I'm talking about guys like Matt Mumford, Chad Bartie, Dustin Dollin and Andrew Currie who in my eyes have all achieved major success in their own unique way. They all did the move to the great skateboard land, California, to pursue their dreams. Some are still there, and others are right back here at home, but they're all making a living doing what they were born to do: SKATEBOARD!

It always makes me proud to be associated with some of the guys who helped to build the Australian skateboarding scene and make it possible for us younger guys to do what we do. I jump at any opportunity to travel or just catch up and skate with them whenever

> *"It always* makes me proud to be associated with some of these guys who helped to build the Australian skateboarding scene and make it possible for us younger guys to do *what we do."*

I can and they remain great mates on and off the road.

In this section I've enlisted the help of a few of my friends, to show you some of their signature tricks. These guys are some of the best skateboarders in the world, so I'm sure you can learn a few secrets from them. I know I have.

Frontside Kickflip
Sydney, NSW

Photo: Dave Chami

DUSTIN DOLLIN } FRONTSIDE KICKFLIP

This trick takes a lot of practice, but when you see people like Dustin throwing them down huge sets of stairs, it's incentive enough to spend every waking hour learning them.

The secret to the frontside flip is all in the foot positioning. The stance you'll need to adopt is similar to a standard kickflip so your heels are off the heel-side edge of the board, but you're slightly tip-toed on both of your feet. Remember, your back foot should be ready to pop and scoop the board around.

When you're ready for the flip, your back foot should pop the tail and at the same time push or scoop it forward so you start to frontside 180.

At the same time as the "pop", your front foot should flick up and off the board as if you were doing a regular kickflip, but this time give it some extra power. This is not only to make the board flip, but to assist in its 180 rotation.

Your whole body should be in the process of turning 180 while at the same time your board is also flipping and turning 180 underneath you. At this point you should hope to have enough pop so your knees are tucked up and your feet are clear of the action.

You should aim to catch your board with your back foot when you're about halfway through the rotation. [Check Dustin's frontside flip over the rail for a text book example of the perfect catch.]

Once your back foot is on board continue the rest of the rotation and get your front foot over those bolts before stomping it down.

If you don't quite complete the 180 degrees; pivot the remainder of the turn on your nose. But for full points and a high five from Dustin it's best to perfect the full rotation.

Switch Heelflip
Melbourne, VIC

Photo: Steve Gourlay

LEWIS MARNELL } SWITCH HEELFLIP

There's something about switch heelflips that just makes them dope and Lewis has one of the best in the business.

Start by rolling switch and position your feet as you would a standard heelflip, only your stance is reversed.

Crouch down with your weight centred over the board in preparation for the pop.

Resist the natural urge to rotate back into your normal stance by keeping your shoulders parallel with your board. Smack the tail down and as you drag your leading foot give the board a solid flick to get the [switch] heelflip in motion.

As the board begins to flip, pull your knees in towards your body; this will get them out of the way of the flip and give you some extra height in the pop.

By now the board should have flipped and be re-connecting with your feet. Aim to keep your feet flat against your board and prepare for the landing.

Just like Lewis here, aim to stomp both feet over the bolts and roll away smoothly, if not slightly camouflaged.

ANDREW CURRIE } FRONTSIDE ROCK n ROLL

This trick is a timeless classic and there is no better person to learn it from than Andrew Currie.

It's not essential, but a couple of good tricks to have dialed before hitting this one are backside rock n roll and rock to fakies.

Confidence is the key here, so man up before pumping up the transition towards the lip. You should approach on a slight frontside angle.

As you reach the top of the ramp, lift your front wheels over the coping and push your board up onto the platform. You want to lock the back wheels against the underside of the coping, so measure that push so your board doesn't fly right out the top of the ramp.

As your back wheels make contact with the coping put the weight onto your back foot and turn your shoulders back towards the ramp ready for the rock back in.

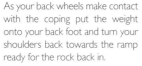

With all the weight on your back foot pivot off your back wheels and turn the board 180 and back into the ramp. Make sure this action is done fast and smooth, as you want to get your front wheels down before you lose control and zing out.

Once your front wheels have touched down, lean forward, absorb the transition, and roll away humming a few bars of your favourite AC/DC song.

Sequence: Home Torti

Frontside Rock n Roll
Canberra, ACT

Try to get your feet centred over those bolts, before stomping it down and rolling away. Then perfect them, until like Chima, you can do them down all things massive.

Keeping your eye on your board, you can now start thinking about the catch. You should aim to catch your board with your front foot before it completes its full 360 degree rotation. You'll still be in the process of turning 180, so make that catch and complete the final stage of the turn with your board under your feet ready to land.

CHIMA FERGUSON } FRONTSIDE BIGSPIN

Once you have frontside 180 ollies and pop shove-its in the bag, why not combine them and add a lesson from Chima, to come up with a banging frontside bigspin.

As you pop your board, push or "shove" the tail with your back foot to get your board on that 360 rotation. At the same time you'll start to turn your body 180.

To avoid the board actually flipping [instead of turning] keep your back foot directly in the middle of the tail when you pop.

Setting up for a frontside bigspin; your foot position should be similar to if you were doing a pop shove-it.

You might find it helps if you crouch a little extra before popping the tail of the board. This will help give you some extra pop and the momentum you need to spin your board the full 360 degrees.

Nollie Flip
Wollongong, NSW

Photo: Steve Gourlay

SHANE O'NEILL } NOLLIE FLIP

Shane spends more time on board than anyone I've ever met. This has resulted in him mastering more tricks than you could throw a chicken nugget at—this is just one of the many he has on lock.

Nollie as you would normally, giving that nose a good crack to get off the ground. As you do this drag and flick your back foot diagonally off the tail of your board.

In principle the motion of the nollie flip is almost identical to a kickflip. The difference is you're going to nollie it instead of ollie it.

Roll along with your front foot on the nose and your back foot placed just in front of your rear bolts. You should be slightly tip-toed with your feet hanging off the heel-edge of your board.

As the board completes the flip catch it with both feet evenly. To make your life easier, when landing a nollie flip you want to avoid your board coming down mob, or boned—keeping your feet at an even level will help to avoid this.

After the catch, stomp it down and consider yourself one step closer to being able to challenge Nugget to a game of S.K.A.T.E.

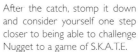

Crooked Grind
Gold Coast, QLD

Photo: Andrew Mapstone

JAKE DUNCOMBE } CROOKED GRIND

Like most tricks, crooked grinds are best done going fast—you won't see Jake doing them any other way.

As you reach the ledge pop an ollie high enough so that your front truck is higher than the edge you're going to grind.

Approach the ledge at an angle similar to what you would assume for a boardslide. It's also worth taking an extra push to gain enough speed to keep you grinding once you lock the crooks.

In order for the board to lock into the crooks position you need to land with your board slightly diagonally and with all your weight on your front foot. Just be careful not to slip into a noseslide. Once you're locked hold the grind, using both your hips and shoulders to balance you through it.

As your foot drags towards the nose with the motion of the ollie, follow through with it and transfer the pressure to your front foot, boning the nose down so that the front truck makes contact with the edge of the ledge.

As you reach the end of the ledge use your front foot to nudge the board out of the grind in a motion similar to a nollie, absorb that landing with your knees, and roll away.

SHANE AZAR } FRONTSIDE SMITH GRIND

The best looking smith grinds are done with control and power. And that's just how Shane rolls —look and learn.

Before heading into the frontside smith it would help if you're confident doing both frontside 50-50s and 5-0 grinds.

Approach the rail as if you were going to do a standard frontside 50-50. A bit of extra speed won't go astray as it will help throw you clear of the rail if the smith grind sticks.

When you execute the ollie leave the 5-0 grinds at the door and instead visualise ollieing straight into the smith position.

You'll need to think about putting the majority of weight on your back foot, while extending or boning your front leg so the nose of your board dips down.

If you've got yourself into the correct position in the previous steps you should make contact with the rail with your back truck and the rail of your board at the same time. Now it comes down to staying parallel to the rail, and maintaining the balance on your front and back foot so you stay locked in to the grind.

As you reach the end of the rail, shift the weight onto your back foot and pop out with an ollie motion. Land, roll away and then go and learn them backside; Shane insists these are much easier if you wear a Manly Sea Eagles scarf.

Sequence: Steve Gourlay

Photo: Andrew Mapstone

Frontside Smith Grind
Melbourne, VIC

THE GAME
of
S.K.A.T.E.

When it comes to games in the skateboarding world one phrase that rings through the streets and parks is "Game of S.K.A.T.E."

This game is based on the classic basketball game called H.O.R.S.E. where the players compete to shoot from different areas of the court—each time they miss, earning another letter of the word. S.K.A.T.E. is the same principle only you compete to land particular tricks. It can be played with as little as you and another mate or with as many people as you like.

Not only is this game a perfect way to kill time, but sometimes it's all it takes to get you over the line to learn that new flat ground trick you have been trying for weeks.

Brush up on the rules, find yourself some smooth ground and prepare to go into battle.

HOW TO PLAY

There are lots of variations in "the rules" and how to play, depending on who you ask, but the principles of S.K.A.T.E. remain the same. Generally when you're playing in a group, the majority rules so it's good to go with the flow.

• One person needs to start the game, so to decide who starts you can play a game of rock, paper, scissors. The winner of this starts the game of S.K.A.T.E. by performing a trick of their choice. Assuming they land their trick, the play then moves on to the next person who must attempt the same trick. This continues along the line until all players have landed the same trick. If any player misses the trick, they have to take a letter ie; the first time you miss a trick you get the letter S.

• When the play returns to the person who started, they then do their next trick of choice and the game continues around the circle again. If the person who starts the game, doesn't land their trick they miss their turn and the next person in line starts the game instead with their own trick of choice.

• Once a player has all the letters; S.K.A.T.E. they are knocked out the game.

• The winner is the player who remains, with the least amount of letters, once everyone else is knocked out.

You don't just need to play S.K.A.T.E. on the flat ground, you can mix it up and play it on a rail or a ledge, or play it switch or only with flip tricks —whatever way you think of to play it, is all good.

N.B If skateboarding on the flat ground is not for you and you tend to lean towards skating transition, there is also a great game for you. We call this game "Add a Trick". This game is great if you are at your local mini ramp with a couple of your mates.

It is as simple as someone starts by dropping in and doing one trick on the facing wall. The next person then drops in and completes that trick then adds one of their own on the next wall. The key to a good game is to start the tricks off simple and get a long line going; half the trick then becomes remembering the line. The winner is the person who can complete the line without falling or forgetting the sequence of tricks.

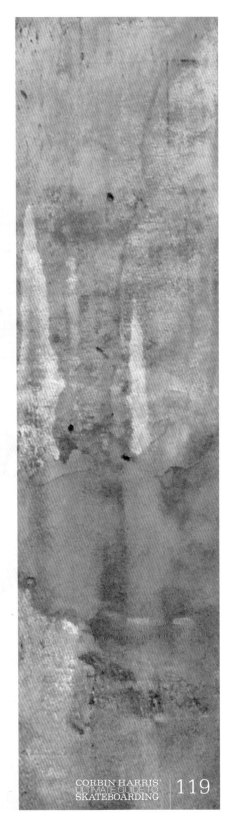

"*Nothing* beats the adrenalin rush of conquering the big stuff; it rates as one of the best feelings you can get *skateboarding*."

Frontside Stalefish
Five Dock, NSW

GETTING GNARLY

STEPPING UP TO THE BIG STUFF

So far I've covered the fundamentals; tricks you can do in your driveway and tricks to learn at your local skatepark. Now it's time to step it up a notch and have a look at a few tricks that will get the heart pounding. Don't worry, instead of throwing you in the deep end I've shot the tricks on smaller and ultimately friendlier obstacles so you can get the hang of it.

Nothing beats the adrenalin rush of conquering the big stuff; it rates as one of the best feelings you can get skateboarding. You'll need your skills up to speed and your confidence in spades to tackle these ones.

So, buckle-up and take a few deep breaths; it's time to get gnarly.

BLUNT TO FAKIE }

The blunt to fakie can be tricky to learn but once you've got them down you can savour them on anything from a street bank to a vert ramp.

Pump up the transition as if you were doing a rock to fakie, but with a little more speed.

Once your front trucks are over the lip, hold a manual for a brief second until your back wheels pass the coping and your tail locks in to the blunt position. The key to the blunt is not to stall it. The whole trick should be one fluid motion of coming up in to the blunt position and popping back out immediately.

There are two ways to pop out of the blunt: you can pop the back wheels in and manual down to clear your front wheels, or you can opt for the ollie pop out to four-wheeled landing (which I am doing here).

Either way you choose to pop out, bend your knees to absorb the landing and roll away.

Blunt to Fakie
Oregon, USA

Backside Tailslide
Five Dock, NSW

BACKSIDE TAILSLIDE }

I have too many favourite tricks to mention, but there's no doubt the backside tailslide is right up there on top of the list.

Roll up the transition at a slight angle, with your feet on your board as if you were going to ollie.

I find the faster you go the more you slide, so pick up the pace when you're comfortable.

When you're just below the coping execute a similar motion to a backside 180 ollie. The difference being, instead of popping above the coping, keep the weight on your tail and scoop it around in preparation for locking in to the tailslide.

As the back wheels make contact with the coping turn your head and shoulders towards the direction you want to slide. At this stage it's important to keep your knees bent, as this will help lower your centre of gravity and make sure you slide as opposed to stopping dead in your tracks.

If the first three steps have gone to plan, you should now be sliding. You can push the slide even further by straightening your back leg slightly and keeping the pressure on your tail. I also find it helps if your back foot is slightly tip-toed.

When the slide starts slowing down, turn your leading shoulder into the ramp and proceed to push into the transition, similar to if you were doing a standard drop-in.

PIVOT TO FAKIE }

The challenge to the pivot to fakie is to get back into the ramp without your front truck hanging up—the day you land it you'll be stoked to go home bruise free.

You can feel this trick out by trying the motion halfway up the transition a few times before taking it all the way to the coping.

Approach the ramp with slightly more speed than you would for a rock to fakie.

Just before the lip, start to turn your body [similar to a backside grind] and eventually let your back truck lock on to the coping. Instead of continuing to turn 180 degrees like a backside grind or pivot, turn only approximately 90 degrees and temporarily stall on your back truck. Your weight should be on your back foot and your shoulders parallel with the coping.

Once you've stalled the pivot it's time to bring it back in fakie. While keeping the weight on your back foot, lean back into the ramp and let the back truck disengage with the coping.

Both your back wheels should now be in full contact with the transition. Keep the weight on your back foot until the front wheels have cleared the coping. It helps to think of it as doing a quick little fakie manual down the ramp.

As your front wheels touch down, ease the weight off your back foot, bend your knees slightly and roll away. Don't worry if you smile when you land your first one, that's completely acceptable.

Photo: Andrew Peters

Pivot to Fakie
Werribee, VIC

Lien Air
Los Angeles, USA

Photo: Andrew Mapstone

LIEN AIR }

Lien spells Neil backwards and is named after legendary pro skateboarder Neil Blender who invented the grab back in the 80s.

This trick should be approached with speed and confidence, so once you've got your frontside ollies dialed on transition, you should be ready to give this a go.

Tap your tail on the ollie just before you hit the coping and really bust out the top. Although you're travelling frontside, the key to this trick is not to carve into it too much; the more up and down you go the better this trick will look.

Once you've launched out over the coping, suck your knees and board up and go in for the grab with your leading arm. You should grab your board just behind your front foot.

Once you have a solid grab on your board, turn your head over your leading shoulder to spot your landing.

Let go of your board ready for landing and start extending your front foot towards the transition.

When landing, stay centred on your board and a little compressed. This way you'll have less chance of zinging out and more chance of throwing up the horns as you roll away.

Sequence: Mike O'Meally

Lien Transfer
Ulladulla, NSW

Photo:Davide Biodani

TO COMPETE
OR NOT TO COMPETE...?

Skating in competitions still gives me the jitters to this day. I almost can't decide whether I love them or hate them … maybe a bit of both. The adrenalin aspect is the bit I love—putting myself under pressure and trying to perform—but even that can go both ways. I've either had a bad day and fallen off, or I've landed a trick in a comp that I've never done before. The thing I don't like is mentally dealing with all the details that run through your brain, like: stance, body weight, what tricks to do, where to do them, who else is doing what, how much time is left on the clock, not falling off … the list goes on. It makes it feel like I'm learning a new sport again, like if someone is coaching you in golf, they'll give you dozens of pointers and you're trying to remember them all to put into that one swing. It can be a case of information overload. To get through it though, you eventually find a "happy place" where you remind yourself that skating a comp is no different to skating a park the way you normally would, and then you let the adrenalin do the rest.

Unlike in professional surfing, competitions aren't as much of a massive feature of pro skateboarding, although skate world tour circuits and international comps definitely exist. It may never become like the surfing comp circuit, as it seems most pro skaters prefer to shoot videos or photos of their skating and put it out there in the skate media rather than in front of a crowd and judges. At a professional level one of the good things about comp skating is it promotes skateboarding and enables people who otherwise wouldn't know anything about it to witness the skills and thrills it incorporates.

On a local level, amateur competitions can be great for building your confidence and meeting new people, including other

> *One of* the best things about comp skating is it promotes skateboarding and enables people who otherwise wouldn't know anything about it to witness the skills and thrills it *incorporates.*

skaters who are at the same level, or a touch better than you are. It's amazing how sometimes just having other people to skate with who might be a bit more advanced than you, will push you to learn much quicker.

If you're thinking about skating in a comp, there's no harm in testing the waters, and if it's not your thing, so be it. With or without competitions one thing I am sure of is that skateboarding is awesome, no matter what context it's in.

FRONTSIDE NOSEBLUNT }

The frontside noseblunt is considered a tough trick to master. It takes equal parts courage and commitment to bring one of these back in successfully.

To take the pain out of learning this one, it would help to have both switch blunt and frontside disasters dialed.

Approach the lip with a similar amount of speed as you would for a frontside disaster.

Pop a small frontside ollie, making sure to keep your weight over the top of the board. As you spot your landing begin to bone the nose of the board down towards the coping ready to lock in to the noseblunt.

Lock in to the coping with your wheels on the platform and your nose over the coping and facing into the ramp.

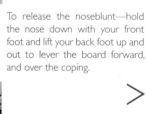

To release the noseblunt—hold the nose down with your front foot and lift your back foot up and out to lever the board forward, and over the coping.

As you pop back in, use your back foot to guide the board into the ramp nice and straight.

Once your back wheels clear the coping, re-adjust your weight over both trucks and compress back into the transition for the roll out.

Frontside Noseblunt
Victoria Park, WA

Frontside Nosegrind
Ocean Grove, VIC

Photo: Steve Gourlay

FRONTSIDE NOSEGRIND }

The fun of a nose wheelie + the sensation of a grind = good times.

Approach the coping on an angle with your body and feet in a position to frontside ollie. Pop your ollie just below the coping. I find you don't need to put too much effort into the ollie as your momentum should help to get you onto the coping.

Once you're above the coping extend your front leg to push your nose down onto the coping. Eye the spot on the coping where you want to touch down.

Once your front truck makes contact with the coping lean into the platform slightly—this should help lock the nosegrind into place. This is where practice comes into it; it may take a few tries to find the sweet lock-in spot. It's hard to explain but once you find it, you'll know, as it just locks and feels controlled.

As you're grinding, you'll find your back foot automatically slides back down the board slightly. When the grind slows down and you want to pop out, this back foot position will allow you to do a slight nollie to get you back out over the coping, and into the ramp.

Make sure your back wheels are clear of the coping, before compressing your legs and rolling back into the transition.

It may take some time to master the timing and balance of the grind and the pop in, but believe me, it's worth every second.

MELON TO FAKIE }

Melon, which is short for melancholy, means to be sad. This trick isn't really, though, and you won't be when you land one.

Once you have grabbed an ollie melon on the streets and put a couple down some stairs or out of a kicker it is time to take it to the transition.

Approach the ramp with ample speed to ensure you get airborne once you hit the coping.

Just before your front truck hits the coping, crack an ollie like you never have before and start flying. As you take off start reaching down with your leading hand in preparation for grabbing the board behind your front foot.

As you catch the board lean back into the ramp and pull the board tight onto your feet. In the same motion straighten your front leg slightly. This will bone the nose and make this trick the gem that it is.

As you feel gravity kicking in this means it is time to prepare for landing. Make sure you are really good at rolling down transition fakie as you are about to drop away from a height. Release your board but make sure you are clear of the coping so as not to hang up.

When you feel your wheels hit the ramp begin to pump into the transition for a smooth roll away.

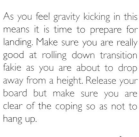

Melon to Fakie
City Park, Melbourne, VIC

FRONTSIDE DISASTER }

A frontside disaster done with ferocity will scare the pants off anyone within 40 metres and might even gain you the title of noisiest dude in the park.

Approach the ramp with more than enough speed to hit the coping, and position your feet as you would for a frontside 180 ollie on the flat.

Lean back slightly and take off on your ollie just before you reach the coping. Start scooping your tail around as you come up out of the ramp.

Keep turning your shoulders so your body follows. Your body weight should stay inside the ramp, while your back leg should extend out towards the platform. With your weight distributed evenly in this way you should land your board centred onto the coping.

As your board smacks down onto the coping, shift your weight to your front foot to prepare for the re-entry.

To re-enter the ramp lean forward, putting the weight onto your front foot. Lift your back wheels over the coping and rock back in. As your back wheels make contact with the ramp distribute your weight evenly and roll away.

Frontside Disaster
Private ramp. VIC

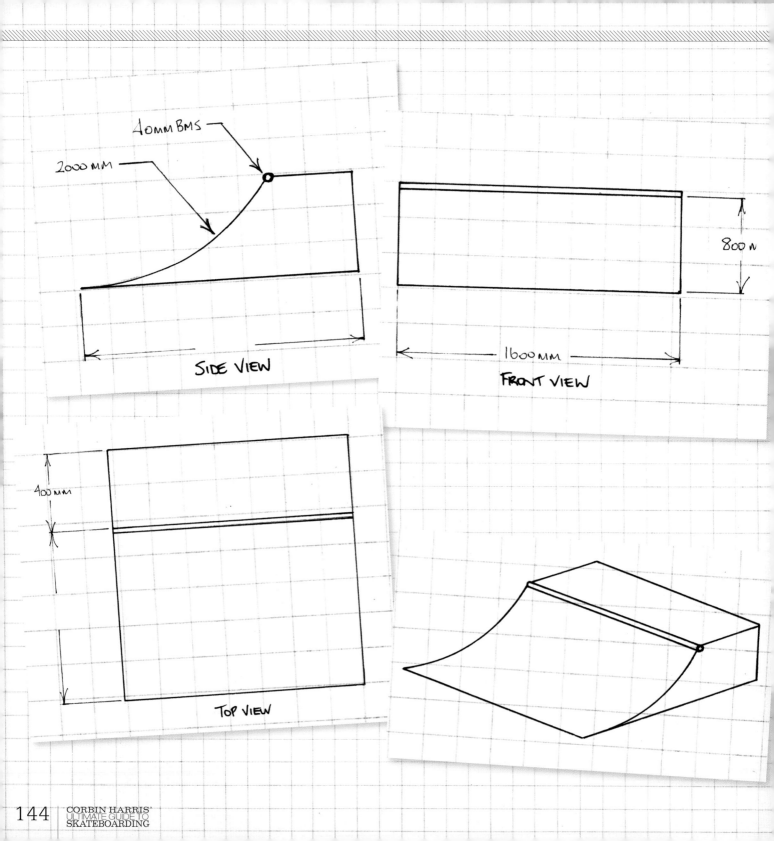

40mm BMS

2000 MM

SIDE VIEW

800 N

1600 MM

FRONT VIEW

400 MM

TOP VIEW

HOW TO BUILD A QUARTER PIPE

Not everyone has the time, space or money to build a half pipe. But there is an easy alternative. It's half the hassle but can be just as much fun. With the right tools and materials a quarter pipe is also much easier and affordable to build than you might think.

As with the ledge, your local hardware store should be able to cut everything to size for you; then it's just a matter of measuring and cutting the remainder of the materials accurately and putting it all together. In no time at all, you'll have your very own backyard training facility and be one step closer to becoming a ramp champ.

SPECIFICATIONS: Quarter pipe 1600mm(long) x 1600mm (wide) x 800mm (high)

MATERIALS REQUIRED:

70mm x 35mm Pine
12 x 1600mm lengths

12mm CD grade Plywood
1 x 1200mm x 2400mm sheet

9mm CD grade Plywood
1 x 1200mm x 2400mm sheet

Coping
1 x 1600mm x 40mm black mild steel [BMS] or galv pipe

Hardware
approx 100 65mm x 8 gauge tek screws
approx 40 25mm x 8 gauge tek screws
2 x 40mm x 40mm 90 degree galv brackets

TOOLS NEEDED:

Battery drill, #2 phillips bit for screws
Hand saw or circular saw if available
Jigsaw
Square
String
Hammer
Tape measure and pencil

1. The first task is to cut out the two side transition templates from the 12mm ply. The trickiest bit is marking out the transition so you know where to cut. Start off with the ply on a flat surface with the long side facing towards your feet. From the left corner measure up 800mm, then using your square, measure in 400mm. This will eventually be the platform.

Now you need to draw out the curve of the transition. This is where you need to concentrate! This quarter pipe has a 2000mm transition, so from the left-hand bottom corner measure 2000mm along the longside of the ply and make a mark. Then at a right angle measure directly up 2000mm (indicated by the yellow line). But this goes off the ply, you say!? Yes, it does, so at this point you need another piece of stable timber that you can put a nail into to mark the 2000mm point. It is important you accurately measure and position the nail as this forms the fixed point from which you'll draw the curve.

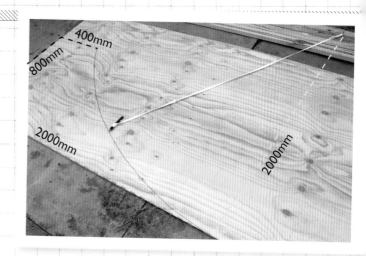

2. So bang a nail at 2000mm from the bottom of the ply then attach your string to the nail. Measure along the string 2000mm and tie a pencil at this point. Keeping the string tight, place your pencil on the 2000mm point at the bottom of the ply (where the blue and yellow lines meet) and in one smooth motion trace the pencil up to meet up with the platform. Your efforts should be rewarded with a nice curved line as seen above.

3. This template now needs to be cut out. I recommend getting an adult who knows how to use power tools, or your local hardware shop, to cut this out for you. If you've got an adult cutting the ply for you, remind them before cutting that the ply needs to be supported far enough off the ground so when using the jigsaw the blade can't hit the ground. If they follow along the lines you've marked out, you should end up with the shape of ply you can see in the next step.

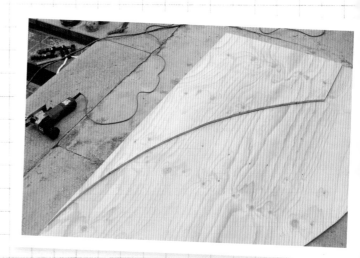

4 With the first side of your ramp cut, flip this template over and place it onto the opposite corner of the same sheet of ply. Now it's as easy as tracing around the template with your pencil and that way you know both pieces will be exactly the same. You can now remove the template and get an adult to cut the second template out for you.

5. Now it's time to assemble the sides you've just cut out. Standing the ply template upright, so the platform section is at the top, take the first 1600mm timber batten and screw it to the back corner of the ply. Then take the other ply template to the other end of the batten and screw that together also. Two 65mm tek screws at each end will do it. You should now have the two sides standing up and starting to resemble a ramp!

6. You can now attach another 1600mm batten to the top of the ply templates and also at the front where the transition starts. The foremost batten should be placed so it sits on the ground and just flush with the curve of the ply. Make sure you're working on a flat, even surface otherwise you could end up with a dodgy out-of-square ramp.

7. Working your way up from the bottom batten you just screwed in, mark out 130mm along the edge of the ply and screw in your next batten using two 65mm screws at each end. Repeat this six times. Make sure you screw each batten in at both ends before going on to the next batten.

8. Once you have the seven battens in place up the transition, it should look like this.

9. The next step is to attach the coping. You first need to notch out the top corners of the ply for the coping to sit in securely. To do this, measure 34mm from the top then 40mm back from the edge of the ply. Now cut it out using a handsaw, or get an adult on the jigsaw if it's easier.

10. To fix the coping into position use the two 90 degree brackets by sliding one end into the pipe then screwing the other end onto the side of the ply to hold it in place. Now the remaining two battens can be screwed into place either side of the coping for support.

11. To complete the platform, the top can be cut from the leftover piece of 12mm ply. The dimensions for the top should be 380mm (d) x 1600mm (w). If you've cut this nice and square to the correct dimensions, when you screw it down it will help bring the two sides of the ramp into alignment. Screw the platform top down to the battens using about 20 of the 25mm tek screws.

12. Now the frame is ready for its first layer of 9mm plywood.

13. Now to prepare the surface of your ramp. Take the first sheet of 9mm ply and lay it flat with the long side at your feet. From the bottom left corner, and the top left corner, measure in 1600mm from the edge and mark the ply. Join these two marks so you have a solid straight line running up the ply in front of you. This is your cutting line, so now get an adult to help you with the cutting. Repeat this with the other sheet of 9mm ply.

14. When fixing the ply, lay it down so the grain of the ply runs sideways; this will help it bend to the curve. Butt the ply up against the coping then VERY carefully apply small amounts of pressure across the sheet until it bends to fit the curve. [It may help to get some mates in here but warn them to be careful not to crack the ply.] Now use the 25mm tek screws to fix the ply to the battens underneath. Space the screws approx 200mm apart across the ramp.

15. To avoid busting any holes in the ramp with your wheels, fix the second layer of 9mm ply over the top of the first layer in the same way.

If you plan to store the ramp out in the weather it's a good idea to give it a few coats of exterior paint. But first it's time to skate!

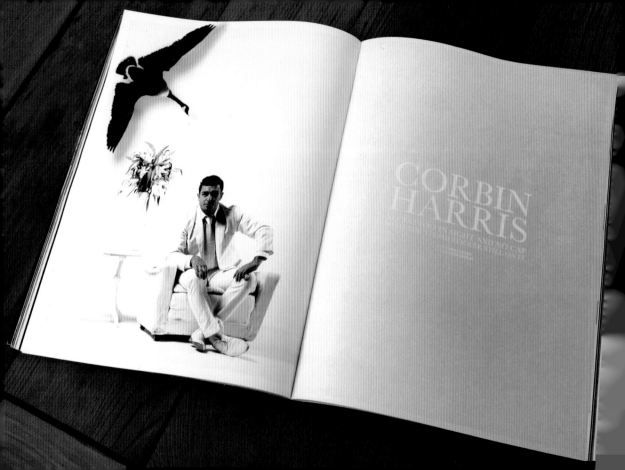

CORBIN
HARRIS

SKATEBOARDING: A CAREER

As a professional skateboarder my job involves much more than just getting photos and footage, or doing comps and demos. This hasn't always been the case, but sponsors' expectations of skateboarders have become much higher over the years. The usual things still apply such as demos and signings, but then opportunities arise, for example, modelling for catalogue photo shoots or working with designers on ideas for new products.

I consider myself lucky to be part of a new era of sponsored skaters, who have more responsibilities as ambassadors for the brands they represent. Like anything, the more you put in the more you get out of it, and in skateboarding, it now means that here in Australia, it's now possible to make it a legit career.

You definitely can't sit around and wait for things to happen, such as getting sponsored; instead, you need to be pro-active and make it happen for yourself. Talent and perseverance will obviously go a long way, but it also helps to have a plan of the big picture of what you actually want to achieve. Skateboarding has given me tons of opportunities, but along the way I've taken courses, such as at NIDA (National Institute of Dramatic Art), which have helped towards my goals to work in television. It's awesome that I can present a show on television that is actually about skateboarding,

> "*Like anything*, the more you put in the more you get out of it, and in skateboarding, it now means that here in Australia, it's now possible to make it a legit *career*."

combining my passions, but be prepared—skateboarding itself will only get you so far.

I often think skateboarding is more than a job, it's a lifestyle, and I'm so fortunate to share that lifestyle with so many amazing people. The people who make up the industry are the people who make it possible for guys like me to skate for a living. The amazing photographers, filmers, team managers, designers, marketing and sales people, retailers, media outlets ... Hey, if a career on the board isn't your thing, there are plenty of great jobs in the industry where you still get to live and breathe skateboarding.

Photo: Steve Gourlay

Sequence: Andrew Peters

Fakie 5-0 Revert
Oregon, USA

ACKNOWLEDGEMENTS

I'd like to say a special thanks to my family: my amazing mother and father for believing in me through some of the hardest times when we never thought we could pull through! My grandparents, Peggy and Pox, and Joyce who are like an extra set of amazing supportive parents. My brother and sister, Shannon and Shawnee, who are awesome. The boys, Kai and EK. And the extended family Nuka, Jet, and Poirot.

Also thanks to Robert and Elizabeth Joske, Shane Moran, Andrew Flynn, Elyse Taylor, Sheree Commerford, Shane Serena, Glenn Scott, Milly Gattegno, Anthony Sedgwick, Brett Chan, Chris Senn, John Respondek, The Robbo's, Sergie Ventura, Trevor Ward, Shauny Eaton, Penny & Toby, Lote Tuqiri, Occy, Bob Burnquist, Vanessa & Raci Gilbert, Jake & Kate, Fergo, Robbie Highlander, Daniel Cester, Andrew Thomo, Kate Ritchie, Robbie Maddison, Chad Ford, Cheyenne Tozzi, Troy Archer, Matt Maunder, Lyndall Wilson, Chris Middlebrook, Kerry Fisher, Mavis Gourlay, Blair Heath, Anthony MacDonald, Richard Penny, Justine Cullen, Morgan Campbell, Colin Blake, Matt Owens, Brett Margaritis & Kris Lye, Ben McLachlan, Dylan Radloff, Adam Howarth, Michelle Glew, Anthony Mapstone, Ryan Wilson, Su Young Choi, Shrewgy, Bruce Robson, Mark Ryan, the Gilbert family, Element, Nike, Red Bull, SDS Surf Dive & Ski, Modus, Hoon, Ogio, Oakley, Ace Trucks, Protec, Convic Skateparks, skateboard.com.au, The Skateboarder's Journal, Slam Skateboard Magazine, Monster Children, the Fuel TV/Foxtel family, everyone at HarperCollins*Publishers*, all the amazing photographers: Steve Gourlay, Andy Peters, Young Vo, Pete Daly, Steve Lightfoot, Rome Torti, Luke Thompson, Jason Morey, Davide Biondani, Mike O'Meally, Andrew Mapstone, and Dave Chami.

To my "mates" who also follow their dream and do what they love, thanks for making the book even better: Dustin Dollin, Andrew Currie, Jake Duncombe, Chima Ferguson, Shane O'Neill, Shane Azar and Lewis Marnell.

Working on a project like this takes a lot of time and some talented people: Steve and Anoushka (Thomo & Coach), Sean Holland and Jack Tarlinton; thank you for all your effort and support. Love ya!

Harper*Sports*
An imprint of HarperCollins*Publishers*

First published in Australia in 2009
by HarperCollins*Publishers* Australia Pty Limited
ABN 36 009 913 517
harpercollins.com.au

Copyright © Corbin Harris 2009

The right of Corbin Harris to be identified as the author of this work
has been asserted by him under the *Copyright Amendment (Moral Rights) Act 2000*.

This work is copyright. Apart from any use as permitted under the *Copyright
Act 1968*, no part may be reproduced, copied, scanned, stored in a retrieval
system, recorded, or transmitted, in any form or by any means, without the
prior written permission of the publisher.

HarperCollins*Publishers*
25 Ryde Road, Pymble, Sydney, NSW 2073, Australia
31 View Road, Glenfield, Auckland 0627, New Zealand
A 53, Sector 57, Noida, UP, India
77–85 Fulham Palace Road, London, W6 8JB, United Kingdom
2 Bloor Street East, 20th floor, Toronto, Ontario M4W 1A8, Canada
10 East 53rd Street, New York NY 10022, USA

ISBN 978 0 7322 9016 0

Cover photographs by Steve Gourlay, back cover portrait by Davide Biondani
Cover and internal design by Jack Tarlinton
Internal photography (unless otherwise credited) by Steve Gourlay
Editorial consultant Sean Holland
Packaged for Harper*Sports* by Thomo & Coach Pty Ltd
Reproduction by Graphic Print Group, Adelaide
Printed and bound in China by Phoenix Offset

128gsm Matt Art used by HarperCollins*Publishers* is a natural, recyclable product made from
wood grown in sustainable plantation forests. The manufacturing processes conform to the
environmental regulations in the country of origin, China.

5 4 3 2 1   09 10 11 12